JOURNEY TO FREEDOM

The Path to Self-Esteem for the Priesthood and Religious Life

James E. Sullivan

PAULIST PRESS
New York/Mahwah

Copyright 1987
by Rev. James Sullivan

Library of Congress Cataloging-in-Publication Data

Sullivan, James E., 1920–
    Journey to freedom.

        1. Self-respect—Religious aspects—Christianity.
2. Spiritual life—Catholic authors. I. Title.
BV4647.S43S85   1987   248.4'82   87-13684
ISBN 0-8091-2905-1

Published by Paulist Press
997 Macarthur Boulevard
Mahwah, New Jersey 07430

Printed and bound in the
United States of America

CONTENTS

Preface   1

Chapter I   Roadblocks to Freedom   3

Chapter II   My World System   18

Chapter III   My Self System   53

Chapter IV   My Perceptive System   73

Chapter V   My Special "Guilt Machine":   107
The Reflex to Blame

Chapter VI   Dismantling My Guilt Machine: 135
The Path to Freedom

Chapter VII   Rebuilding Self-Esteem: 142
Free at Last!

PREFACE

The ideas presented in this book are the fruit of twenty years of individual and group counseling with over two thousand priests, religious and laity at the Religious Consultation Center of the Diocese of Brooklyn. In those years I experienced a great deal of psychic pain, both in myself and in these very special people who trusted me to share their struggles.

In working with them I had two very strong feelings. The first was an almost overwhelming sense of privilege to be there with them and for them. The second was a strong feeling of anger that persons who were so good should feel so poorly about themselves. Their poor self-concept had not only caused them ugly feelings of depression and anxiety; it had also put them in an internal prison more confining than one with iron bars!

Gradually it became more and more clear to me that the human person, just like the human body, is made up of various systems which interact upon each other and depend upon each other. A deeper understanding of these psychic systems, I felt, would certainly be a help to those who feel this imprisonment of a diminished self-esteem. And there are many!

The chapters in this book represent a summary of these psychic systems as I see them. They were first presented in a briefer form at a Mental Health Day for Major Superiors in the Bishop Molloy Retreat House in Jamaica, New York, on November 2, 1983. They were so well received at that time that I decided to rewrite them as a book for priests and religious in general. My earnest hope and prayer is that these ideas will point out the path to freedom for those in psychic pain.

I am very grateful to Justine Johnson for her painstaking care in typing the manuscript and to the other members of the staff for their encouragement and helpful suggestions.

For the purpose of preserving confidentiality, I have changed the names of the people I have cited as illustrations and also some unimportant details.

I have also used in most cases the masculine pronoun for both men and women. This was done only to avoid the constant repetition of "he" or "she," "him" or "her." This procedure is not meant in any way to imply an inequality between men and women, a viewpoint I have never held.

CHAPTER I

Roadblocks to Freedom

Freedom—A Rare Quality

Michael, the middle-aged priest who sat across from me, was a picture of psychic pain. His facial features were taut and tense, his body rigid. When he spoke, it was with evident effort as though breathing was something very difficult for him.

"I feel so awful," he said, in a tone of voice that revealed his great pain. "I'm only in this parish for four months but I feel as though I'm going out of my mind."

He hesitated. "Jim, the pastor is crazy! He raves and rants through the halls like a lunatic. He thinks that we're out to get him. It's like living in an asylum."

Guilt feelings came over him then. "I feel like such a baby! I should be able to take things like this without feeling sorry for myself!"

"Mike," I said, trying to ease some of his pain, "a situation like this would be hard for anyone to take."

"I know—but I'm always telling others that they should accept God's Will cheerfully—I feel like such a damn hypocrite!"

The neurotic atmosphere in the rectory made Michael severely depressed. Prudence and common sense told him that he should ask for a change, but he could *not* get himself to do that. This was the real tragedy; he wasn't free. He was the "prisoner" of an old and distorted spirituality. "This is where the Bishop assigned me," he said. "So it must be God's Will that I stay here and put up with this situation."

I tried to explain that such a spirituality was really the error of Quietism—the false doctrine which held that we must never do anything for ourselves, but simply remain passive and endure all that happens to us. "Mike," I explained, "Quietism was condemned. God expects us to make prudent decisions for our life, not just sit back and expect Him to do everything for us."

It was no use! At least not right at that time! The old perceptions, which were engrained in him for years, were not to be changed with a few words. It hurt me to see how very *unfree* this fine priest could be. He was being destroyed emotionally and yet he could not allow himself any avenue of escape. He was a prisoner, just as really as if he were surrounded with iron bars.

Unfortunately, Michael's situation is not a rare one. All too many of us are surrounded by roadblocks of guilt and inhibitions which keep us from traveling the highway to happiness and joy.

"Live Free or Die"

The state motto of New Hampshire is very appropriate: "Live free or die!" It expresses concisely what most of us human beings feel deeply—that life without freedom is not worth living; more, life without freedom is in itself a special kind of dying.

As far back as recorded history can take us, the ideal of freedom has always been a cherished dream. A handful of Greek city states stood up against the overwhelming might of the Persian empire in order to preserve their democratic way of life. Spartacus led his fellow gladiators in an impossible challenge to the mighty Roman Army, just to breathe for a little while the fresh air of freedom. Heroes like Galileo went to prison rather than compromise their intellectual freedom or recant the free expression of truth as they saw it. And two centuries ago a small band of American colonies pledged to the cause of liberty "their lives, their fortune, and their sacred honor." "I know not how others may feel," Patrick Henry summed it up, "but as for me, give me liberty or give me death."

The desire for freedom is so strong that the very work itself conjures within us delightful images and feelings; images of wide-open spaces without fences or barriers; of snow-capped mountains, majestic and tall; of waterfalls splashing and cascading like music;

images of dancing freely, of singing and playing without anxiety or fear; feelings like joy and happiness and peace.

Freedom is so attractive because it is the right to *live my life* the way *I* choose to live it; to think my own thoughts and express them openly, to make my own decisions and carry them out without fear or punishment. It's the right to choose my own place to live, my own kind of work, to choose my own friends, to pull my own strings. To be genuinely free is to be truly alive.

Not an Absolute Right

It does not diminish my love for freedom when I realize that it is *not* an irresponsible fight, not a right without boundaries. Without limitations, freedom would become *license* and lead to nothing except anxiety and pain.

If you are to enjoy the blessings of freedom, then my right to be free has to *end* where your right to be free *begins*. I have a right to speak freely, for example, but I do not have the right to defame your character or to abuse you in any way by my speech. I have no right to hinder your freedom of choice or destroy your property. If I did have the right to invade your space and interfere with your life, then you would also have the right to interfere with mine! In that case, neither one of us would be free.

Freedom is a right that necessarily involves obligations and the maturity of impulse control. My rights must end at that point where your own rights begin. But, within those boundaries of my own space, genuine freedom gives me the power to live, to work, to choose, to reach out to others with my love, to let others touch me with theirs—all of this without fear, without pressure, without dread of danger or punishment.

True Freedom Is From Within

The longing for freedom is perhaps most often pictured in terms of freedom from external controls and pressures, a democratic form of government in contrast to the repressions and controls of a dictatorship, a safe environment in distinction to a lawless society where right is synonymous with might.

In our preoccupation with this external freedom, we are liable to forget that the most satisfying and life- giving freedom is *internal freedom*—freedom from pressures and roadblocks that are within ourselves. This is the truest and most exalted of all freedoms—and the hardest to achieve. Bishop Ford could be locked in a Chinese prison for years and yet be wonderfully free, free in mind and heart. The contrary is also true! Millions of Americans can enjoy the blessings of external freedom and yet *internally be slaves!* Slaves to alcohol. Slaves to drugs. Slaves to neurotic patterns of feeling and acting! Slaves to torturous feelings of neurotic guilt and masochistic self-punishment! Slaves to live styles that they hate. For most of us the areas of unfreedom in our lives are vast!

The goal of this book is to help us become aware of our internal slaveries, to revitalize the thirst for internal freedom, to help us to get started on our journey.

I am the only one who can achieve internal freedom for myself! Civil laws can protect me from undue interference from *other* people. Unfortunately, no law can guarantee me protection from *myself*! My worst prisons are the prisons of my own making, my darkest dungeons, the dungeons of my own fears and inhibitions and oppressive feelings of neurotic guilt.

Civil law gives me protection against slander and libel. And when I am the victim of this kind of injustice, the court system offers me opportunities for defense and retribution. But who can protect me from the unjust accusations which I impose upon myself? From the merciless punishments I put myself through by my neurotic guilt?

The police force can make me relatively safe from robbery and bodily harm but the army and police force together cannot make me be kind and compassionate to myself.

The truth is that very few of us enjoy *internal* freedom, especially those of us who are religious and priests. For most of us there are a whole series of interior roadblocks which litter our path to happiness and self-fulfillment.

Mary is a typical example. She was very attractive both in her appearance and in her personality. She liked men and apparently men had no trouble liking her. She had a nice sense of humor and real warmth.

But Mary would not let herself get "serious" with any man. She seemed to allow herself just so much enjoyment on a date, and only a limited amounts of dates a month. It wasn't that she didn't long for marriage and a family of her own. On the contrary, marriage was her constant dream.

The roadblock which kept her from fulfilling her dream was her neurotic guilt. She had a twin sister who was emotionally and physically handicapped. Her sister constantly compared herself to Mary in outbursts of self-pity. Mary had everything; she had nothing.

In her *mind* Mary knew that she was not to blame for her sister's misery, but in her *feelings* she felt terribly guilty that her sister was so depressed. So she couldn't give herself permission to have a steady boyfriend. Each time she enjoyed herself on a date, she experienced that painful self-blame that she was "selfish." There was no lack of opportunity in her world; there was only lack of internal freedom.

Walter was another example. He was evidently distressed when he spoke: "Bernie got the job," he said. "I tried my best to be big about it. I smiled and congratulated him, but inside I was hurting, hurting a lot! You know, I don't think the boss *even considered* me for it!"

"This sort of thing happens to me all the time. Everyone else gets the breaks! I just wish that something would break for me—just once!"

Walter was a soft-spoken man in his early thirties. He was shy, self-effacing, the kind of person who seemed to get lost in the woodwork. He was probably right in thinking that the boss had not even considered him for the promotion. Walter seemed almost not to be there!

Situations like this are *not* unusual. Many of us are unaware of the forces within ourselves that infringe on our freedom. We tend to see freedom only in terms of the lack of exterior pressures. Thus happiness and self-fulfillment seem to depend only on *external* factors over which we have little control or no control at all. Therefore, self-fulfillment becomes mostly a "matter of luck." You just have to "hit it right," "know the right people—people who can open doors for you." Things work out for the lucky ones. The rest of us just have to suffer.

We take a very big step forward on our journey to freedom when we are able to explode this myth! While there are *some* obsta-

cles to self-fulfillment that come from without, most of our roadblocks really come from within.

Many Kinds of Roadblocks

My unfreedoms can be of many kinds. Some of them are inhibitions, which hold me back from doing things that I know are good
for me. I know, for example, that reaching out to others on my job
will help create a friendly atmosphere. I'd love to do it, but I'm
afraid. What if they don't like me? I'll probably be an annoyance to
them.

So I don't reach out. Unconsciously the only signals I give are
signals of aloofness, distance, not caring. My fellow workers naturally react negatively to these signals. In their eyes I seem to be
someone who acts superior and uninvolved—so they send back the
same kind of signals to me. They don't reach out either. By now I'm
convinced that I'm in the "wrong job" with the "wrong group of
people." Wouldn't it be great if I worked in a place where people
were friendly and outgoing! Why don't I ever get a break? I don't
even suspect that it was I who started the whole process!

Sometimes my roadblocks are compulsions. Say, for example,
I feel that you have hurt me. The things you said, your tone of
voice, your gestures—they could only be interpreted as a "put-
down." I feel a strong compulsion to "tell you off." My mind tells
me that this is not the right time nor the right place for such a
confrontation. You're too occupied right now. You cannot possibly
hear me.

No matter! I've *got* to get those rotten feelings out of me. My
compulsion burns like a hot coal in my chest. So I blurt it all out!
It's a mess. You can't hear me. You cannot see my point of view.
That's not what you meant at all, you say. You're hurt that I took it
that way. What do I think you are—an insensitive boor!

I feel so frustrated. In my mind I'm playing my old tapes. It's
all *your* fault, I'm thinking. First you put me down. And then
you're not adult enough to admit it. You go and get defensive on
me. You deny the whole thing. If only I worked with people who
were understanding! Sadly, I have no awareness of my own contribution to the misunderstanding. I feel that the entire frustrating
incident was caused from without.

At times it is my attitudes and prejudices that keep me alienated and unfulfilled. No sense making friends with women, I say to myself. All women are deceitful. They smile to your face and then stab you in the back. Why go looking for pain. And how can I trust men? They're all competitive and power-hungry. They are out to beat me and put me down; they're not interested in becoming my friend.

All these distortions, of course, are part of the "baggage" which I carry from my early life experiences. They are not obstacles from *outside* myself; they are roadblocks from *within* myself. I'm not living in a totalitarian regime where lack of freedom is imposed upon me by the government or the secret police. Almost all my unfreedoms are my own "stuff."

The "Prison" of False Attitudes

Take Mark, for example, a man in his mid-thirties, tall and good-looking; he had a lot going for him. He was also bright and sincerely empathetic with other people.

Despite these advantages, Mark was quite depressed. He lived alone, cooked his own meals, and ate alone. People seldom called him. He had almost given up hope that he would ever develop a deep relationship with a woman.

He tried hard to connect with others, went to dances often and invited his dancing partners on dates. After a few dates, however, the relationship was over. He'd withdraw from them.

In spite of all his talents, Mark was *not* internally free. There was a hidden agenda, an unhealthy attitude about women that severely hampered his ability to relate to them.

History taking revealed that Mark's mother was a very domineering and manipulating person who almost completely overshadowed and controlled his father. She ran the family. Mark's father seldom spoke up to her. He quietly acquiesced and took the line of least resistance. Mark did the same, but not without great hidden hostility and pain.

Gradually in counseling Mark came to realize that he saw *all women* through the filter of this experience with his mother. His unconscious attitude was that women were manipulators, were domineering and controlling. Getting close to a woman seemed to mean putting oneself into her clutches. It seemed to involve the abandonment of self-direction, the loss of self-respect. For Mark there was no in-between. Either a man put himself through hoops to please a woman or else he paid the bitter price of rejection and pain. Relating with a woman was clearly a "no-win" situation.

All this, of course, was below the level of consciousness in Mark. Consciously, he only knew that he was very lonely, that he longed for the intimacy of a love relationship. He had no idea at first that another part of him, his insecurity and unconscious fears, were working just as feverishly at destroying relationships as his conscious self was working to establish one.

The moment a woman said anything that sounded like an order, something clicked within Mark. He found himself "freezing" inside. Sometimes he reacted by saying something sharp and sarcastic. Other times he just became very silent and withdrew.

One occasion was particularly sad because the woman apparently was someone who would have been an ideal friend. She apparently found Mark very attractive and wanted to know more about him. They had gone out a few times and she experienced Mark as very present to her, but he said very little about himself. She tried to reach out to him: "Mark you seem so guarded. I'd love to know more about you!" It was a very gentle and sincere expression of interest.

But not for Mark! Immediately the warning button clicked inside him and a filter of "mother" snapped into place. He heard her request as a *put-down*, as blame. With a very evident tone of annoyance he replied, "What you see is what you get! This is me—no more, no less. If you don't like it, too bad!"

She felt crushed. She couldn't talk at first. Tears welled up in her eyes. Another bad signal for Mark. "Here comes the manipulation!" he said to himself. "No way am I going to fall into this trap!" He got up, said "Good- night" and left.

When Mark talked about this encounter in his next counseling session, he was absolutely convinced that she was just "another one of the controlling dames who love to run your life for you." He was like someone on the back of a train that was pulling away from the platform and he swore that the platform was moving away from him.

Like many of us who desire intimacy so strongly and find

difficulty making friends, Mark's main problem was not other people. His chief roadblocks were within himself.

The Roadblock of Guilt

Unfortunately, there are many sources of unfreedom. One of the most devastating is the roadblock of guilt. Satisfying my needs can be fairly easy for me if I can do so without blaming myself for doing it. I can take some time for myself, for example, enjoy a good book or movie, seek out people I really like and spend time with them, refuse to be pressured into projects that I find distasteful. I can do these things with ease when I can do so without any guilt or self-blame. But satisfying *any* of my needs becomes all too painful whenever I feel that I am *selfish* for doing so.

Sister Rosemary was an example in point. She was the principal of a school in a very deprived neighborhood. Through her efforts the school had become a model. She was able to attract very fine and dedicated teachers who were more influenced by her sincerity and professionalism than they were afraid of the neighborhood. She put in long hours in fund-raising; she organized volunteer workers to clean and repair the school, besides the task of supervising the curriculum. She was tired but she had a real sense of peace and accomplishment.

Her real troubles began when her older sister's husband died and her sister showed up "bag and baggage" at the convent insisting that Rosemary care for her. She was "sickly" and could not work. She expected to be waited on hand and foot. When Rosemary tried to convince her to get into a home for the elderly, her sister wouldn't even listen. "I will kill myself if you make me go!" This threat was more than Rosemary could take. She let her stay at the convent, even though her own blood pressure went sky high because of the constant demands and aggravation.

Her friends were furious. They tried again and again to show Rosemary how her sister was manipulating her. To no avail! Rosemary felt unbearably guilty even when others discussed the possibility of putting her sister into a home. Externally she was a free person, a very creative person. Internally she was in a prison, locked up by her poor self-esteem and her dread of feeling more guilty.

The Compulsion To Prove Oneself

High on the list of our un-freedoms is the feeling that I'm always on trial, the feeling that I *have* to perform up to the highest standards in order to prove that I'm worthwhile. This roadblock also begins within me, with a feeling of poor self-esteem. I feel that I am inferior. That hurts so much that I set out to prove to myself and to you that I am *not* a washout. But the only "proof" I can believe is the proof of a performance that is *absolutely superior*. I have to be the very best, or else I'm convinced that my first evaluation of myself is true—I'm the worst!

Such a compulsion is a relentless burden on my back. I never seem to get free of it. No matter how superior my performance may be, it never really convinces me that I'm all right; it only relieves momentarily the feeling that I'm not a disaster.

Dominic, a priest in his late thirties, was a striking example of this kind of compulsion. He worked terribly hard to the point where he couldn't allow himself to enjoy a full day off each week. Occasionally, he'd go out to lunch or dinner with a friend, but he always had to get right back for appointments. He pushed himself unmercifully. He lacked the freedom to enjoy life. He could not give himself permission to unwind and relax.

History taking revealed that as a boy he felt overshadowed by his father. His father was apparently a very unusual man. He was a talented musician and formed his own orchestra as a sideline. He worked his way up in his company from a clerk to vice-president in a matter of fifteen years. People would not speak of Dominic as "Father Dominic"; they would speak of him as "Mr. R's son."

Dominic's mother and sister idolized his dad. So did Dominic! However, his admiration for his dad became a comparison between himself and his dad, a comparison that made him see himself as vastly inferior. It was a terribly painful feeling, a mixture of anger, jealousy, inferiority, guilt! There was only one way he could feel better. He had to be superior also! He had to be the kind of "super-man" that he pictured his dad to be, more so now that his dad had died and was immortalized in everyone's eyes. The area of Dominic's un-freedom was huge. He was a driven man.

It took a lot of time in counseling for Dominic to reach the emotional conviction that there was *no race* between his dad and himself. He couldn't ever be his dad! He didn't have to be! He and his dad were not even on the same track! All that he had to do to be a great success was to be *himself*.

Roadblocks All Around Us

There are obstacles of all sorts that hold me back from enjoying life and finding self-fulfillment. Fear is one of the worst: fear of closeness, which holds me back from loving you or letting you love me; fear of rejection, being convinced in my mind that once you really get to know me, you will certainly not like me and pull back from me. As much as I long and crave for love with my whole being, such fears become like stone walls which hem me in and keep me isolated and lonely.

Fear of failure is another huge roadblock. I see failure as a "proof" that I am inferior. Once I see it that way, even the possibility of failure has to be removed. It would be too much of a blow to my self-esteem. So I don't even try to develop my talents. I can't fail if I don't try, I tell myself. What I *fail* to tell myself is that I also *cannot succeed* if I don't try. And my talents remain buried in the sand.

Often enough the fear of failure is so strong that I will undertake a project and then *make* myself fail (unconsciously, of course) just to get it over with. Actually failing, as painful as it is, is easier to live with than the awful fear that I am going to fail.

Sister Nancy experienced this sad phenomenon with almost an entire class. She dreaded taking this particular fifth grade because all their previous teachers spoke of them as "horrors." They were very unruly and did extremely poorly in their work, given their level of intelligence. Sister Nancy wanted to know why. She was very quiet with them at first, waiting until they stopped their acting-out and finally sat down. When she finally had their attention, she tried to explore with them why they acted the way they did. She finally discovered that a teacher in the second grade had convinced them that they were "no good." They were sure that they could never amount to anything, so they didn't try. They became the failures and discipline problems that they were "bound to be" no matter how hard they tried.

Sister Nancy felt a deep empathy for them. She realized that they were more "sinned against than sinning" and with the kindness and gentleness that marked her whole manner, she led them to such a sense of self-esteem and class unity that their performance and their conduct took a radical change. She removed the awful dread of failure and set them free.

Self-defeating patterns of behavior become roadblocks for many people. Marilyn had cringed as a child when she saw her mother physically beaten by her dad again and again. She literally shook with fear in her father's presence. She hated the nights he came home drunk. Unfortunately, her image of married life was the picture she saw in her own home. She married the *same type of man* as her father and the thirty years of her marriage have been a living hell.

"I know I'm a fool to put up with it," she said. "Everyone tells me that I should leave him, but I can't! I know that they are right, but I just can't! I don't know what I'd do!"

There are probably few roadblocks as frustrating as the *addictive* behavior of alcoholism or drug addiction. In my mind I can see clearly that each drink is a nail in the coffin of my relationships. I'm causing my family and friends unbelievable pain. I hate myself for it! And yet I reach out my hand compulsively and take another drink.

I know that, when I get started on drugs, I'm started on a down-hill road, away from love, away from life. I know that it's going to take larger and larger doses to give me the thrill until I've passed the point of no return and I end up as a junkie in a dark alley. And yet I buy my little package of coke and hurry home to take it. I'm not free.

Oftentimes my roadblock is an inability to be compassionate to myself. I fall and get hurt. The pain is great and I'm inconvenienced by the awkward cast. But I cannot be gentle with myself or treat myself with compassion. On the contrary, I blame myself. It's my "own stupid fault" for trying to ski.

If someone else broke his leg, I'd be very sympathetic and kind. Poor guy! What a tough break! I'd wait on him hand and foot. I'd sympathize with his inability to ski or play golf for many months. I'd give up golf myself in order to be with him and keep him company.

But, when it is *my* leg that is broken, the bottom line is that I was simply a damn fool for taking foolish risks. What was I trying to prove anyway? "You try to show off," I yell at myself, "so now pay the penalty!" I am merciless in my self-blame. I give myself no quarter.

Worse still, I don't let anyone else touch me with compassion either. When they reach out to me with gentle concern, I block it. I change the subject or tell a joke! I'm *unfree*! Unfree in an area that is awfully important for my happiness, the area of gentleness and reverence for myself.

The list of my unfreedoms could go on at great length. I have the money for a new suit but I can't allow myself to "waste that money on myself." I have a chance to go on vacation with a great group of people, but there's too much work to be done. I'd be too upset lying in the warm sun while there was so much unfinished business back home. I can sleep until ten o'clock. There isn't a thing that has to be done before that time, but I'm up at six-thirty. Sleeping until ten just has to be self-indulgent!

Common Denominator—Lack of Self-Esteem

The list is almost endless. Each one of us, I suspect, with a little reflection could add any number of examples from our own life. Our lives are cluttered with roadblocks, obstacles, dead-end signs, each one blocking off huge areas of love, joy, self-expression, self-fulfillment.

When I look more closely at my unfreedoms, it soon becomes clear that there is a basic common denominator to which they can all be reduced, a basic, central root from which they all spring, and that is the awful psychic pain of looking down on myself, the pain of a low self-esteem!

Psychic pain is that *unique* type of pain that I feel when my *sense of self* has become diminished in any way. It is pain that arises from my inner world.

All other pain, whether physical pain or emotional pain, is the result of distress in my outer world. I experience a physical pain in my body or I feel emotional pain about the people in my life. It may be the pain of loss of a loved one or separation from places and people that I cherish. It may be the pain of anger, hurt, or frustration from the way people treat me. These pains come from my outer world.

Psychic pain is the result of distress in my *inner* world. In psychic pain my painful feelings are about *myself*. I feel varying degrees of *revulsion* for who I am and what I am. I don't like myself. I feel stupid, inferior, inadequate to cope with the problems in my life. I rate myself as a "loser."

Sometimes I feel helpless, trapped, incapable of directing my own life or pulling my own strings. When I see myself this way, I feel like a puppet, pulled and pushed by others, manipulated by their expectations and demands. I'm a "nobody!" I'm trapped in an internal prison from which there seems to be no escape.

No other pain strikes so deeply at my person than this psychic pain of self-hate. No other pain is so potentially destructive to self-fulfillment and happiness. Lack of self-esteem is the core of almost every other roadblock on my journey to freedom and fulfillment.

It is precisely because psychic pain strikes at my innermost core that it robs me of internal freedom. I want to reach out to love, but I am afraid to do so. Who would want me as a friend? What do I have to give! People may be nice to me but it's only because *they* are *good*, not because I am lovable. I'd be a terrible bore for them.

And how can I develop my talents? I'm convinced that I don't have any real talents. Any attempt to achieve in the academic world would end up in failure. I'd only make a greater fool of myself! Bad enough to feel the way I do now without adding more fuel to the fire of my self-depreciation.

Other types of pain can often be transformed into a growth experience. Physical pain can certainly deepen my realization of the pain of others and increase my compassion for them. I can mean it when I say, "I know what you are going through. I'm awfully sorry!" Emotional pain in the loss of a friend can be united with the suffering of Jesus and make me realize more completely how much I need him in my life. It can be the sword which opens up my heart to a deeper prayer life, a deeper love for Him.

The pain that is most difficult, however, and *almost irredeemable*, is the psychic pain of a diminished self-esteem. It is almost unsalvageable because it robs me of my inner freedom.

If I were to experience real affirmation and love, it would be a great boost to my self-esteem. But there's the rub! Because I don't have self-esteem to begin with, I have a huge roadblock which *prevents* me from experiencing affirmation and love. It's a vicious cycle. You give me ample evidence that you love me—but I simply cannot believe it, cannot accept it or let it warm me. I'm so convinced that I am of no worth that you cannot possibly love me. You just don't know me! If you did, you'd see for yourself that I'm a washout.

The Purpose of This Book

The number of my unfreedoms is sizable and the restrictions that they impose on my life are devastating to my happiness and fulfillment. Almost all of them, at least all of my internal roadblocks, have their central root right here, in the psychic pain of my disgust for myself.

The journey to freedom, therefore, must also begin here, with an understanding of psychic pain, how it began in me; why its hold on me is so powerful; what I can do to overcome it, to regain and enhance the true vision of myself. "You shall know the truth and the truth shall make you free." Once I see myself as He sees me with my *true* and *genuine worth*, I shall have a beautiful sense of self-esteem. Then I shall truly be free. The journey to freedom is the path to self-esteem—a journey of faith.

CHAPTER II

My World System

Self-Fulfillment—Satisfying My Needs

My human heart is a hunger—a hunger to be understood and loved by at least one other human being. Just to know that another person has entered my private world of thoughts and feelings and looks out at the rest of the world as though he or she were looking through my eyes, and says to me: "Yes, I understand how you feel. I don't blame you for feeling that way. You're not bad because you feel that way. You're *human*, that's all!"

Just that comforting presence in my world of feelings is deeply satisfying to me, even if the other person cannot lessen the pain that I am feeling! Even if he cannot remove the obstacles that are frustrating me, or cure the cancer which is eating away at my body. Just the fact that he understands what I am going through, that he cares and feels it all with me, just that makes me feel less alone, less foolish, less confused, less guilty. My whole being hungers for that kind of understanding.

And when that special person goes beyond understanding, beyond care for me as a person, when he sees me as this *unique* person that I am, sees in me qualities that draw him to me and make him want me as a friend, then my joy is complete. I'm not only understood. I'm cherished. I'm loved. One of my deepest human needs has been met.

In being present to me and understanding my feelings, he gives me the love of charity and proves to me that he is good. When he

18

sees my special individual qualities and desires to be my friend, he proves to me that *I* am good.

He and I then begin the process of entering a new relationship. Now there's a new interest between us, a new understanding, a new rapport and responsiveness. Where before we were both lost in a sea of human faces, now we stand out to each other—as though spotlights suddenly illumine each of our faces. We stand out for each other now above the crowd. There's a new joy when I hear his footstep, a new expectancy, a new interchange, a special sensitivity in picking up each other's feelings and meanings. There's a new warmth and closeness that brings great joy to both of us. A bridge has been built; a relationship has been born!

Self-fulfillment is this special happiness I enjoy when such basic human needs of mine are satisfied. My eyes are fulfilled when they can see color and form. My ears are happy when they are able to hear because that is what ears are made to do. And if a watch had feelings, it would be happy when it was telling time accurately. The same is true of myself as a person. Fulfillment is the journey's end, the actualization of my full potential as a human being, the inexpressible joy of *being fully* and *completely* what I was made to be!

My absolute and perfect fulfillment, of course, will come only with the possession of God Himself in the beatific vision. At that moment every one of my needs will be so completely satisfied that my only desire then will be to spend eternity basking in the unveiled loveliness of Beauty Itself.

Fulfillment in this life has to be a limited and relative fulfillment. I can never completely be at rest in this world, never completely satisfied. The most enjoyable job will always have something lacking; the closest and most meaningful relationship will never quite be just enough. Fulfillment in this life is always a journey. I never quite reach the goal until I possess God in heaven.

While I cannot reach the final goal in this life, nevertheless it is here in my present life that I have to *begin* my journey. I never quite reach the goal until I possess God in heaven. But I can achieve a relative fulfillment to the degree that I succeed in satisfying my needs, the needs of my outer world and the needs of my inner world.

My World System

My world system may be defined as the sum of all my needs in relation to the world and people around me. It encompasses all that I need to *give* to the people around me and all that I need to *receive* from them. Fulfillment and happiness for me depends in large part on how free I am to give to others and how free I am to receive from them.

My first needs obviously are my physical needs, those which sustain my physical life. These are fundamental because if they were not fulfilled even for a short time, I would die—and then I would not be capable of any other kind of activity.

I have a need for fresh air with its life sustaining oxygen. Without it, I would probably die or suffer brain damage in as short a time as five or six minutes.

I also have a strong need for sleep. I could live without food and water longer, much longer than I could live without sleep. Sleep is so primary that, if I were forcefully kept awake for two or three days, I would begin to hallucinate. I'd have a psychotic break, hear voices that were not there, see sights that didn't exist.

Water is probably the physical need which is next in importance, followed by the need for my body to have food and the ability to eliminate waste products and fight infections.

Finally, I need a certain amount of privacy and solitude. This need is probably felt in different degrees by different people. However, some amount of solitude is needed by everyone. I probably would experience a similar psychotic break if I were deprived of all solitude for an extended period of time.

Some of the religious Sisters, who were imprisoned during the Freedom Marches in Alabama, found the lack of solitude to be the worst pain. They were never alone during the entire length of their imprisonment; never without the oppressive invasion of noise, except for a few hours of sleep at night.

These physical needs are probably so fundamental that no other satisfaction could possibly substitute for them. Even though Mahatma Gandhi found great personal satisfaction in fasting in order to end the factional conflicts in India, nevertheless his body suffered a terrible deterioration from his fast. If he had not put an end to it, he certainly would have died.

While my physical needs are my most immediate and fundamental needs, they are probably the easiest for me to fulfill, at least in our country. The United States has been blessed with prosperity and external freedom. There is no real lack of fresh air or food or water. And most of us do not experience severe inhibitions about getting enough to eat and drink or getting enough rest and solitude.

Expressive-Assertive Needs

Unfortunately, the same cannot be said for my next set of needs, my expressive-assertive needs. Too many of us, especially those of us in religious life and priesthood, suffer some rather severe inhibitions here.

My expressive-assertive needs include first and foremost a need to ventilate my *powerful emotional feelings* to a person who really listens and cares. My feelings of anger, frustration, disappointment. My joyful feelings of elation, excitement, enthusiasm. My sad feelings of loss, pain, hurt, rejection. All these feelings are *charged* with energy, like electricity flowing from a dynamo. They have to be released.

Holding in explosive feelings like these is like stopping up the spout of a kettle and not allowing the steam to escape. The pressure builds up and up, until eventually the entire kettle blows apart!

The same thing happens in my body when I hold in my strong feelings. The energy of those feelings, the expansive, explosive energy has to be released in some way. When I don't express those feelings *outwardly* with appropriate words and affect, then their energy usually turns *inward* and literally *batters* my body, causing all kinds of psychosomatic disturbances, symptoms such as ulcers, high blood pressure, stroke; debilitating conditions such as diverticulitis, diverticulosis, asthma and arthritis. All these are the result of bottled up feelings of trapped energy. The smothered energy either attacks my body in this way, causing those painful physical conditions, or else it finds another "escape" in neurotic, self-defeating behavior, such as over-eating, excessive drinking, sexual acting out. Sometimes the avenue of escape is in the form of sarcastic speech or an abrasive manner that can severely injure and even destroy my relationships.

Sister Mercedes was an example of this kind of displaced energy. She came for counseling at a time when every muscle in her body was taut and tense. She felt that she was about to lose her last friend in the world and that prospect caused her to feel intense anxiety.

The intake interviews and early sessions revealed a woman of strong feelings, feelings which she felt had no legitimate outlet for expression. She had a dedication to justice and fairness and would get very angry at injustice. But anger was not a "legitimate" feeling for a religious woman, so she continually stifled it. Such suppression, however, didn't last very long. The pressure would build to such a pitch that it would break out explosively.

Sometimes the explosion took the form of compulsive masturbation. When it did, she felt awful about herself. She experienced dreadful feelings of depression and low self-esteem.

At other times the explosion took the form of angry outbursts, outbursts that were often much greater than was appropriate to the incident which triggered them. The built-up pressure of her anger was so great that the moment there was the slightest release of anger, all the past anger came spewing forth with it. These outbursts only came occasionally, because they would be followed immediately by terrible remorse and a new all-out effort to suppress all new angry feelings. However, they were frequent enough to make most of the other Sisters very afraid of her, and they kept her at great emotional distance.

Sister Mercedes had only one true friend who stuck with her through thick and thin—until the time when she also experienced Mercedes' anger bursting out against her. She was frightened and terribly hurt. She told Mercedes that if that ever happened again, their friendship was over. She simply could not take that kind of abuse!

The tears streamed down her cheeks when she told me this. I felt very deeply for her. Here was a sensitive and loving woman and she would allow herself no healthy outlet for her intense feelings!

In the course of counseling she was able to see that she had limited herself to only two extremes for handling her feelings—the extremes of suppression on the one hand or destructive outbursts on the other. She learned that in reality she had many options, many healthy outlets through which she could express her feelings with adequate affect and clarity, outlets in which she could feel understood and accepted, and even loved for her honesty and genuineness.

Once she began to express her hurt, without attacking the other person, she felt a sense of relief that she had not felt before. She got the other Sisters to understand *how* she felt and *why* she felt that way. And the symptoms of compulsive masturbation, muscle tenseness, and violent outbursts, all collapsed like a house of cards.

The truth of the matter is that I have *no choice* whether or not to discharge my emotional energy. The energy simply *has* to be discharged! Either it is discharged in a healthy way through adequate words and appropriate feeling expression (affect) or it gets turned inward and then invariably it gets released in a destructive way.

My deepest expressive need is to *feel free* to ventilate this powerful emotional energy, free to uncover it and let it out in a healthy way, thus easing the explosive pressure within me.

The Need for a Listener

In order for me to feel free to express these feelings adequately, i.e., with enough force so as to depressurize my body, I have to have someone special present to *receive* my feelings, someone who will *not reject them*. Simply letting them out when no one else is around does not do me much good. I can try this. I can yell and scream and punch a pillow, but very little energy is released in this way. I can clean the house with the speed and energy of a whirling dervish; I can walk at a furious pace thinking, "I'll walk it off!" If I'm a teenager, I can even blast my radio until the windows vibrate. All of this lets out a little of my pent-up energy, but does not give me the relief or satisfaction that I need.

I need understanding. I need care. I need someone who will respect my need to talk, someone who will hear me through without constant interruptions or comments, empty clichés—someone who will accept my feelings with reverence, who will understand and care! This is the only release of my explosive energy that is truly de-fusing and satisfying.

Without such a person in my life, it is too frightening for me even to consider letting these feelings out. When I'm at the boiling point in my feelings, I simply *can't bear* to have anyone tell me that I *shouldn't feel this way*. That only makes me feel worse!

In one of the most painful incidents in my own life, when I felt betrayed by a friend, I felt the strongest need to talk out my pain with a fellow priest. I was hurting like a toothache and I just needed him to understand and feel it with me. Unfortunately, I chose the wrong "listener." Apparently he was so intent on appearing neutral that he kept on telling me how good my former friend really was and how sure he felt that this man never really meant to hurt me; how I must be mis-reading the whole incident. I'm sure he meant well but those things were just about the last things in the world I needed to hear at that moment. I felt immeasurably worse. I couldn't get him to understand that I was bleeding. I had to stop and hold the feelings in. It was like a nightmare.

It is also too painful for me to spill out this sacred part of me, my inmost feelings, only to be told, "That's stupid to feel that way! You shouldn't feel that way." This too is unbelievably painful! So painful, that if I suspect that you're going to tell me this, I simply will not let you know my feelings. I'll hold them in no matter how high the pressure builds.

When I'm hurting like this, I don't need a *lecture*. I don't need advice or comments. I need a listener! I need a friend who will enter my world with me and listen and listen and listen; listen with his ears and with his eyes and with his heart! A friend who will *understand* how awful I feel and let me know that he understands, a friend who will reassure me that in no way am I bad because I have these strong feelings. I'm human, that's all!

Airing my feelings is very important for my physical and mental health. But I usually cannot do it until someone gentle and understanding sets me free. I'm usually so ashamed of my strong feelings, especially those that I view as negative feelings, that I'm afraid you will despise me if I let you know them or what is almost worse, that you will give me a lecture!

When I experience your ability to enter my world and sense your refusal to be judgmental and harsh, when I experience your reverence which allows me to be myself and feel my feelings without your offering any unwanted comments or advice, then in a very real sense you set me free! I can now let all the charged up feelings come pouring out! I don't have to be guarded and defensive. I don't have to watch my words. I don't have to hold back the tears. You treat them all with reverence. The terrible pounding pressure is relieved.

Even when my powerful feelings are happy, joyful feelings, I still need you as a listener to accept them. A feeling as pleasant as joy can be painful when I have no one with whom to share it. If I've received a great honor so that I'm practically walking on air, the joy of it can turn to dust unless I have a caring person who will be happy with me. Someone who will appreciate how much that honor means to me; who can be almost as enthusiastic about it as I am.

It's not sufficient to honor myself to treat myself to a drink or a good dinner, to give myself the luxury of reviewing it over and over again in my mind. Joyful feelings are explosive, expansive energy, the same as painful feelings. They can only be de-fused in the loving, enthusiastic presence of a caring person.

Angry Feelings

Perhaps the most frequent of all my strong and explosive feelings is the feeling of anger. Anger is a feeling that is very difficult to express well! Probably this is so because it is a distasteful feeling. Anger is an *impulse* on my part to *hurt* you in some way—or at least to push you away from me—because I feel that you have *hurt me.*

It doesn't matter what the hurt might be. It may be an insult—real or imagined. It may be my perception that you are ignoring me, not listening to me when I talk. It may be embarrassment, frustration. It may be some physical pain that you caused me. It may even be the pain of loss when I feel that you are rejecting me. Whatever the pain may be, the moment I feel the pain, I immediately experience the response—the *impulse* to *hurt you back.*

Since this is so—that is, since anger is the immediate response to any feeling of pain or discomfort—it is evident that angry feelings are probably the feelings that I experience most frequently. On the average day I suffer numerous discomforts, the annoyance of traffic, the hurt of discourtesy, pressures of all kinds. I'm subject to misunderstandings, to slights, to sarcastic remarks. I experience excessive heat, cold, rain, snow, dead batteries, clogged streets, burnt-out fuses. I'm the victim of frustrations, demands, put-downs. Each of these discomforts gets me angry to some degree. It may be a slight reaction; it may be a very strong one—but every pain or annoyance triggers off *some* degree of anger in me. The truth is that I have to deal with my anger very, very often!

Anger is also one of the most *difficult* feelings for me to express in a healthy way—probably because anger is a desire to strike out at you and hurt you, or at the very least to push you away from me to an emotional distance where you cannot continue to hurt me.

Most of us—especially those of us in religious life and priest-hood—are very uncomfortable with this kind of feeling. I don't like to think of myself as a person who wants to hurt others. That seems to me to be un-Christian and makes me feel ugly and guilty simply for feeling such an urge. It is mainly this uncomfortable feeling of shame that makes anger one of the most difficult feelings for me to handle well. And yet, like all my other strong feelings, I have to get it out or it will fester inside of me.

Anger's Many Disguises

One of the clearest proofs of how difficult it is for most of us to deal with anger is the evidence that anger wears a hundred different masks—all of them an effort to hide my anger not only from others but even from myself. Silence very often is anger—that cold, sullen silence which is a refusal to talk to the person who has hurt me; an unwillingness even to discuss what went wrong.

Not looking at you is another disguise for my anger— for my anger or for my fear. Looking into your eyes is an invitation to openness, a willingness to share, an openness—even a desire—for intimacy. When I am angry with you and not ready to talk it over with you as an adult with an adult, then I feel a strong *inhibition* from looking into your eyes. I don't want openness between us. I don't want interaction. I want closure. I want distance.

Anger often wears the mask of a look that could kill. Eyes that glare, lips that are tight, facial muscles that are drawn and stiff—all these are designed to let you know that you should feel guilty and ugly and absolutely ashamed of yourself. It's my way of hurting you, of getting even with you.

Anger sometimes wears the mask of sarcasm—sharp and cut-ting remarks; sometimes the look of apathy—the look that says loud and clear, "I couldn't care a damn what you think or say or do!" And I'm hoping that you get that message. I'm hoping it makes *you* feel terrible!

Anger can even wear disguises that, to the untrained eye, look like pleasantries. Singing and whistling can be anger. The translation is: "I'll show you that you can't get me down!" Politeness and agreeableness: "Oh yes, you're *so right*—yes, yes, yes, yes, absolutely!" The translation is: "Will you please shut your mouth!" Like the over-politeness of the angry recruit who salutes sharply and says, "Yes, sir, sergeant, sir!" with such emphasis that it is meant to go through the sergeant's heart like a bayonnet.

Anger Must Be Discharged

Masking my anger in one of these ways is an effort on my part to avoid the "shame" of my anger. However, masking it does not really defuse it. Most of my anger still remains inside me like scalding-hot coffee that burns me with ugly physical symptoms. I develop headaches. I have "blah" feelings. I'm tired, disinterested. My blood pressure begins to rise, my stomach gets acidic even when there is no food for it to digest. The acids begin to work on the stomach itself and I begin to develop an ulcer.

As ashamed as I may feel about being angry, I simply have to get my anger out of me through a healthy release or else suffer these dire consequences.

How can I defuse my anger? I have only three avenues for the release of these explosive feelings—and unfortunately two of these three are inadequate and self-defeating.

The first avenue is the road of attack, the way of aggression. You've hurt me—or I feel that you have hurt me—so I hurt you right back. I don't act with self-control and discipline. I *re-act*! Spontaneously I lash out at you, strike you in some way—physically or by words; I put you "in your place." I "tell you off!" All this before I know for sure whether you really *intended* to hurt me; before I know for sure whether I really understood what you did or what you meant!

This avenue of counter-attack is a temporary release of my explosive anger but it is neither a healthy release nor a lasting release—*No one wants to be attacked*! So, the moment I attack you,

you become furious and want to attack me back. And if you give in to that urge, the same as I gave in to mine, then we only end up screaming insults at each other. Instead of our anger lessening, it only continues to increase in its fury. —Acting out my anger in this fashion is almost always self-defeating and almost always injurious to you. We'll consider later on how such attacks can cause immeasurable damage to your self-esteem. Whether my expression of anger is a direct attack, a put-down, sarcasm, a hateful look or an indirect attack, such as coldness and emotional distance, a refusal to talk to you—it all adds up to the same thing. It is a *devaluation* of your worth as a person, a terrible hurt to you which makes you only want to hurt me back. Attacking you may offer me a momentary release—but almost surely it is followed by more pain for me and great hurt for you.

Holding Anger In

Most of us in religious life and priesthood understand that acting-out our anger is not the Christ-like way to act nor does it bring about any real relief or reconciliation. Those times that we may have slipped into the pattern of attacking others or putting them down only caused us added grief and remorse. We may have even permanently alienated our loved ones.

The big temptation therefore for most of us is to go to the opposite extreme and to *hold in* our anger, to suppress it by turning it back inside. There is no *explosion* but there certainly is *implosion*! The explosive energy of my anger releases its force against my internal organs, just as if I swallowed a lighted fire cracker and it exploded inside me.

The effects of such implosion on my body and my feelings follow very quickly. The first and immediate effect is a feeling of depression—a lessening of self-esteem. I find myself feeling very low at times like this. Almost nothing interests me. I want to sleep a lot and yet my sleep is fitful and restless. Food becomes tasteless and unattractive. I don't eat a regular meal; I nibble at it. Even sexual desires are dulled. Nothing is stimulating or exciting.

The depth of my depression of course depends on the intensity of the angry feelings that I'm suppressing. The greater the anger, the deeper my depression. The less intense the anger, the milder my depression. However *some* degree of depression almost always follows when *I* hold in my anger. Depression might well be described as nothing more than swallowed anger.[1]

Even when my depression is caused by a feeling of guilt, the same dynamic is at work. Guilt is really anger which is directed inwardly, directed against myself. When I feel guilty, I am angry at myself, I'm disappointed with myself. I blame myself. When the guilt is severe, the feeling I have about myself is one of absolute *disgust*! All these feelings are an expression of anger. They are outlets of explosive energy which is geared to hurt, only the target *now* is not others; the target now is myself. I despise myself. My self-esteem suffers a direct attack with the immediate effect of depression.

Psychosomatic Symptoms

Depression of itself would be more than sufficient "punishment" for this mis-management of my angry feelings, but it is far from being the only effect on my body and psyche. A second result of swallowed anger is the formation of psychosomatic symptoms. Since my anger *implodes* and crashes with its full energy against my internal organs, I experience considerable discomfort and damage internally. Often I develop severe headaches from this "underground explosion." It is relatively rare that headaches are caused by a tumor or other organic disturbances. Over ninety percent of headaches are caused by internalized anger.

Other psychosomatic symptoms are ulcers, diverticulitis, diverticulosis, disturbances to my gastro-intestinal system. Sometimes the "weak" point which gives way before this implosive energy is the cardio-vascular system. I develop high blood pressure, a condition that is quite serious, because when it lasts too long, it causes enlargement of the heart and in some cases a rupture of the arteries in the brain leading to a stroke.

Suppressed anger sometimes causes stuttering and stammering. I want the anger to come out and yet I'm afraid to express it. So

---

[1]In very rare cases depression is due, not to repressed anger, but to a chemical imbalance in the body. For these persons anti-depressant medication is needed and probably will continue to be needed in some form for years—somewhat similar to the way insulin is needed for the diabetic. However, apart from these relatively rare cases of chronic depression, most depressions are reactive depressions—the result of swallowed anger.

my speech becomes like a motor where some of the spark plugs are firing and others are not. It sputters and coughs rather than running smoothly.

At times my respiratory system is the weakest link in the chain which breaks before the suppressed energy of my anger, and I develop breathing problems like asthma. This is a frightening condition. I simply can't seem to breathe at times—as though some huge vacuum sucked up all the air and there is none left for me.

Suppressed anger can even upset the chemical balance in my body resulting in the very painful condition of arthritis. It can rest in my fingers or wrists or elbows, any one of my joints. They get red and swell, and any movement or contraction causes me great pain. It is probably most painful of all when it rests in my spine. Then, almost any movement of my body results in a pain that is excruciating.

Slush-Fund

Swallowed anger can not only cause these physical symptoms but it builds up within me an ugly emotional slush fund, a fund of unresolved nasty feelings like resentment, moodiness, bitterness. I feel sour and irritable, even when time passes and I no longer remember the original reason for my anger! The unreleased energy still boils within me seeking for some avenue of escape. Unfortunately it often gets out *sideways*, so to speak, in nasty remarks and comments. I become sarcastic and cutting. My facial features become hard and cold, my tone of voice sharp and biting, my body language negative and distant.

I'll never forget a priest I knew years ago who was typical of this sour personality. A group of us were on vacation at the priest's camp. We prized sunny weather more than gold because all of us loved golf. This particular year it rained eight days in a row; it was awful. Then the sun broke out and our spirits lit up like a Christmas tree. One of the old German priests put up his hands in exaltation and said, "Ah, what would the world be without the sun!" He was echoing what we all felt, except Walt, the sour one. Walt called out, "Ah what the hell is the world even with the sun!" I could hardly believe my ears! After eight days of steady rain he couldn't appreciate the sun.

That's the way the slush-fund makes people! Walt had been bitterly disappointed about some early assignments and he had never dealt with that anger. It all built up inside him like snow and slush that has been trampled on and kicked around in the streets. He *always* looked mad. His tone of voice was constantly raspy and sour. It was painful to be in his presence. Just to experience one person like Walt would convince anyone that swallowing anger is the least desirable way to handle it.

Talking It Out

The only healthy way for me to defuse my anger is to *talk it out*; to express my pain to you who have hurt me. I need to express it with clear and appropriate feeling so that you have no doubt how much I am hurt. I need to use a tone of voice that reveals the amount of pain I feel and facial expressions that let you understand in no uncertain terms how I am hurting and why I feel that way.

You've hurt me by what you said or what you did, or by what you failed to do. You have caused me to bleed. I need to show you the blood! You have to be made aware of the effect that your gesture or neglect has had upon me. This is awfully important. For me to feel relief from this explosive energy of my anger, I have to know that you understand how deeply I have been hurt.

I must not attack you! I must not blame you or heap abuse on you—even though my feelings urge me to do so. I've been hurt so my first impulse is to lash out at you and hurt you back. I can't help *feeling* that way but I must *not* give in to that feeling, firstly because an attack upon you only makes *you* angry and terribly complicates the difficulty between us. Now it is twice as hard for us to find a reconciliation.

Secondly, I must *not* attack you because I don't know for certain whether you really *meant* to hurt me. I may be completely mis-reading your words or actions. There is only *one* thing I really know for certain and that is that I feel very hurt and angry. So *that* is the feeling that I should make known to you. "Wow, do you really mean to say that I'm stupid! That makes me angry!" I don't *know* conclusively that this is what you meant, so I have no right to attack you. All I know is that this is how your words *sound* to me, so I tell you how I hear you and how I feel.

Then you can deal with my feelings. If you did not mean to imply that I was stupid, you can clear that up. You can say, "I'm awfully sorry that you heard it that way. I don't mean that at all! I only meant to say that this one word may be misspelled—that's all!" Once I hear you clarify what you really meant, I no longer feel put-down. I am no longer angry.

When I tell you in a gentle way how I have heard you, you don't feel threatened or angry. You simply feel sorry that I mis-read you and that your words have caused me pain. And you are quick to reassure me that no hurt was intended. It is fairly easy for us to resolve the anger and to feel close to each other again.

No One Wants To Hurt

There isn't one of us who wants others to hurt us. That's almost self-evident. What might not be self-evident is that few if any of us want to *hurt others* either. Usually the only time that we want to lash out at others is when we ourselves have *first* been hurt by them. It is seldom, if ever, that a person is so mean- tempered that he starts out to hurt others for absolutely no reason.

And yet there *is* a lot of hurt in our lives and consequently a lot of anger. What we need to realize is that *most often* it is the result, not of a deliberate intention to hurt, but the result of misunderstanding. I bring my own "bag of worms" to each encounter with you and I tend to hear your words with the meaning they have for *me*—rather than hearing them as you intended them, with the meaning that they have for you! Because I misunderstand you I am hurt. It's not that you *set out* to hurt me!

So, for example, you tell me that I've gained some weight—meaning that I look healthy and good. But I'm oversensitive about my weight (my "bag of worms") so I hear your words as though you were saying that I look fat and sloppy—that hurts me. I get angry. —But that's *not* what you meant. Your words were complimentary. It was *I* who took them as a disparagement and a put-down.

This is why *talking out* my anger is *the* healthy way to deal with it. The moment I say "Ouch, that hurt!" you're able to understand how I heard you and you can clear up my perception immediately. "Oh, I'm sorry! That's not what I meant. I think it's good that you put on a few pounds. You look great!"

Learning how to express my anger in this gentle way is the key to dealing with the most explosive of my expressive needs. Many a marriage could be saved if couples learned how to defuse their frustrations and hurt in this way; many a friendship would be preserved!

Need for Meaning

My second expressive-assertive need is one that has deep roots in my human nature. I need to feel that my life makes sense. I need to know that my life has meaning: proximate meaning, here and now; ultimate meaning— meaning that lasts into eternity.

I have a longing, if I'm honest with myself, for prestige. I need to know that the people in my world consider me to be a person of worth, someone whose life makes a difference. It's hard on me to be "lost" in the crowd, to be considered just another person. When I think that people see me that way, I feel an awful emptiness. I need those around me to appreciate me as *someone special*. I long for my neighbors and fellow workers to see me as a *person of worth*, as someone who makes a real contribution to their world.

It is hard for me to fulfill this need if I do not have real job satisfaction. If I feel that my role is not an important one, that the "real action" is in working for social justice, then I feel poorly about myself—even though my teaching, objectively speaking, is forming many young hearts with ideals of justice. And the same is true when I feel that being an associate pastor is the "bottom of the barrel!" I don't feel that I'm someone special. I feel like a clod.

A number of priests and religious feel unfulfilled this way. They feel that they have *never* been *appreciated*—never been called forth by their Bishop or their community, seldom, if ever, acknowledged for their talents, never selected to be a principal or a local superior or the head of a department. That kind of hurt runs deep!

Before Vatican II we priests and religious had a real sense of prestige simply because we belonged to that privileged class which was admired and esteemed—certainly by all Catholics and to a large extent even by the non-Catholic world. We were "*the*" authorities on religion, morals, right-living. We were "the" noble people.

An unfortunate by-product of Vatican II's exaltation of the role of the laity and its praise for the dignity of marriage is that the role of priests and religious seemed to be diminished in importance not only in the eyes of the laity but in the opinion of priests and religious themselves. Many priests and religious today, far from feeling a sense of prestige, are asking themselves: "What is our meaning today?"

Many retired religious feel a similar distress. Their self-image unfortunately was built in large part on how much work they did and how much they accomplished. Now that they are retired and "have it easy," they no longer feel special. "How can I be a person of worth when I am not 'doing' anything constructive and helpful to others?"

This feeling flows partially from a false indoctrination that their worth lies in our deeds rather than our person. And partially it is due to a failure to find meaningful "work" befitting their retirement years.

We could be of immense service to our older priests and religious if we helped them appreciate how much their wealth of experience means to us. How their *presence* and *care* does more to enrich us than any active work they might perform.

I need job satisfaction, role satisfaction. I need to sense that I am appreciated, that my life makes a difference in my world.

Secondly, I need to feel that my life has *ultimate meaning*. I need to feel that I'm living my life for a *purpose beyond myself*. I need an anchor in eternity!

It would be unbelievably painful for me to think that this life is all that there is. There is so much injustice and cruelty in this life— so much pain that doesn't seem to make sense or be for any purpose. Without faith life in this world seems like a "dog eat dog" existence, as though we were all caught up in the hands of some blind force like a tornado—caught up, tossed around and smashed to the ground—without purpose, without meaning. —If that's all that life was it would be just too much to bear!

These were exactly the feelings of Jacques and Raissa Maritain, the famous French philosophers in the early part of our century. They were so disenchanted with life here on earth, after witnessing the carnage of World War I, that they actually made a suicide pact. If they could discover no ultimate meaning for their lives, they wanted to end their lives.

Fortunately for themselves and for the untold thousands whom they eventually touched by their exemplary lives and writings, it was at this point that they met the famous Dominican theologian, Fr. Garrigou-Legrange. He introduced them to St. Thomas Aquinas and his Summa Theologica. The vision which that gave them of God's love and God's plan of salvation just thrilled them with hope and meaning and literally transformed their whole lives.

A strong faith in God is not only a religious blessing for us; it is a psychological boon as well. We religious and priests may have problems with our other needs, but at least with this need most of us do not have any serious difficulty. We *know* that we were made for eternal life. We may not feel that our Bishop or our Superior General knows that we exist, but *Jesus* knows and Jesus cares, and that means an awful lot!

Love Needs

My third set of needs are the needs of my sexuality— my love needs. Probably no other needs of my world system mean as much to me as these. Their fulfillment brings me a wonderful sense of intimacy and joy. Their frustration leaves me terribly lonely and empty.

Sexuality is God's gift to me in order to end my loneliness. "It is not good for man to be alone. Let us create for him a helpmate like himself." Gen. 2, 18.

In creating me a sexual being, God gave me both the need and the power to end my loneliness by relating to you in love. I have within me power to make the most perfect of all gifts, the gift of myself. This *gift of self* is the heart and core of all love.

My need to love is on three different levels. Each level involves the gift of self. The difference between each is a difference in the degree to which I give myself. Each successive level demands a deeper investment of myself. Each deeper investment brings me a greater fulfillment and joy.

Charity

The first level of love is the level of charity. This is the kind of love that I can have for all people—whether they are attractive or not. When Jesus commanded us to love everyone, it is of this love of charity that He was speaking.

The part of myself that I give to you on this level of love is my *outer* self. I give you my care, my sensitivity, my interest and concern. I listen to you. I enter your world, show you that I care. I respond to your needs as best I can.

My *motive* for loving with this love of charity is not necessarily your beauty or goodness. You may not look beautiful to me. You may seem grouchy and irritable and distant. My motive for loving you with charity is your *dignity* and worth as a person—a person for whom Jesus died. Because I'm aware of your dignity and worth, I reach out to you with sensitivity and care. I give you the gift of my outer self.

On this level of charity I do *not* share with you my inner self— my innermost feelings. That sacred part of me is reserved for the next two levels of love—for my friends.

Love at this level of charity is the fulfillment of that part of my sexuality which is my *parent role*. God created me in order for me to give life, to nourish, to protect, to help others to grow. I cannot feel complete as a human being until I fulfill this role in *some way*. Just as my eyes cannot be fulfilled unless they see and take in the world around me in color and depth, so also I cannot feel fulfilled as a person until by my love *I give life* and nourishment— until I help you to find yourself and to be yourself.

Some time ago I invited Charles, a new client, to take part in a group which met weekly at the Center. He declined at first. He said that he was so depressed that he could not possibly listen to anyone else's pain. I said to him: "Charley, I realize how awful you feel— and I'll certainly respect your wishes if you'd rather wait until you are feeling better—but ultimately you *have* to make yourself listen to others and be concerned about them! Otherwise, you'll never really *find yourself*."

He looked perplexed. I went on to explain: "You were created to relate to others with reverence and love. You can never really find you or be you until you learn to care for them!" He did prefer to wait for a while but he understood what I meant.

We priests and religious usually fulfill this need very well. The realization that our sensitivity and concern can touch people so deeply and help to relieve their pain, that realization usually moves us very much. Our problem here is more often in the opposite direction, i.e., we often are *overly giving* of ourselves to others to the point where we neglect to give to ourselves. We forget that Jesus said, "Love your neighbor *as yourself*" —not "instead of yourself!"

Sometimes priests and religious face another problem with this need to live a life of charity. In our complicated age, when the helping professions have become so sophisticated and specialized, there are some who feel terribly inadequate for the task of counseling their parishioners who are anxious and depressed. They feel that they are not properly trained to understand people's problems or to help people who are in distress. It's not a lack of willingness on their part. It's just that they *feel inferior* and often that feeling holds them back from even trying to help people.

As a result they not only find it difficult to reach out to others with sensitivity and concern, but they often suffer some psychic pain as well. They look down on themselves. They consider themselves to be lacking as Christians. We priests and religious in particular cannot be happy about ourselves if we are not helping others in their need.

Friendship

The second level of love is the level of friendship—that very special emotional love which is a most fulfilling experience. Friendship is the relationship of mutual love between peers. In friendship I not only give you my outer self; I also give you my *inner self*—my deepest, innermost thoughts and feelings. In friendship I share with you who I really am.

The motive for this most extensive gift of myself is my emotional response to your beauty and goodness. I like you! I like the way you think and talk. I like your warmth, your sincerity, your generosity. I see *more* in you than your dignity and worth as a person. I see the beauty and goodness of this *individual person* that you are. And because I'm so attracted to you, I want you also to be attracted to me. So I not only listen to you with sensitivity and care, I also let you know who I am and what I'm really like. I begin to reveal to you my inner self. And if you respond to me in the same way as I have responded to you, then something truly beautiful is born—that very special love-relationship of friendship.

The experience of real friendship is one of the most exhilarating experiences that I can have in this life; one of the deepest needs of my world system. It is not an exaggeration to say that friendship is absolutely necessary for happy and qualitative living. Someone has put this very succinctly when he said: "There is no life until one has truly loved and been loved, and then there is no death!" I can *exist* without friendship. I can move about and work, but I cannot really *feel alive*!

And yet all too many priests and religious do *not* feel free enough to have a very dear friend! The same is true of many lay persons. It just seems to me to be more ironical and more sad in the case of priests and religious because their whole life is devoted to love. They give and give of themselves and yet there is very little return of emotional love in their own lives. Their students and parishioners will show them gratitude on occasion but they don't have the security and joy of knowing that they are very, very special in someone's eyes. They never feel cherished! And so in their own inner life they are lonely and empty—and hurting like a toothache!

Friendship is the fulfillment of the second role of our sexuality—the *companion role*. Because we are sexual beings we have the need and the power to enter into a deep relationship with someone we dearly love. We have the *ability* to make friends but unfortunately, all too many of us do not have the *interior freedom* to make friends. If someone we liked reached out to us, we could respond with great joy and become loyal and trustworthy friends—but our shyness and fears tie us up in knots and prevent us from initiating a relationship.

I'd love it, for example, if someone I liked were to call and ask me out for dinner, but I can't call. I feel almost sure that others wouldn't want to go out with me. They might be polite and say "Yes"—but in their hearts they'd feel trapped. They'd find me boring, and they'd be very anxious to have the evening end quickly!—It's a torture for me to feel this way. The anticipated rejection is just too much for me to bear. —So I hold back. I don't reach out to others. —And I'm left to myself—alone and really hurting!

John, one of our young priests, told me that he was so anxious to develop a few good priest friends that he spent two years trying to explore the possibility of such a relationship. During that time he reached out to over a hundred priests who were within his own age bracket. He invited them to go out for a day together or to join him for dinner. He shared with them his ideals and feelings about priesthood and Church and asked them to share their feelings in the hope of discovering common ground, mutual interest, mutual attraction.

The results were terribly disheartening for him. Out of the approximately one hundred priests he went out with, only two expressed any interest in a deeper relationship and one of those already had a close friend and couldn't promise John much of his time. John told me: "I never realized how many wounded and isolated men we have in the priesthood." He discovered that the vast majority of the men he had reached out to were lonely men. They were hard workers and most of them were trying very hard to be good priests.

On the level of *charity* most of them were exemplary men. They gave of themselves unstintedly in their ministry. —But they themselves were lonely and unfree. They longed for closeness but dreaded the risks!

Even trying to arrange a single day out was a difficulty for John. One week he called up twenty-two priests to get a companion for his day off. Of that number, all except three were unable to make it at all. And the three who could meet him could do so only for a couple of hours. It wasn't that John was a distasteful kind of person that others would understandably avoid. The opposite was true. He had an absolutely engaging personality, a sparkling sense of humor and a depth of sincerity seldom found anywhere. And yet even a very personable man like him found it very difficult to have his expressive needs met. His fellow priests were too caught up with their hectic schedules or turned off by fears and inhibitions.

Genital Love

The third level of love is that of genital love. When a man and a woman experience love at the level of friendship, they both experience in a particularly strong way their need for genital satisfaction. They not only give to each other their outer self and their inner self; now they long to give to each other their whole self— their body as well.

We priests and religious are no exception to this urgent need and desire for genital fulfillment. By our vow of celibacy we make the will act and commitment not to enjoy genital satisfaction, but this act of the will does nothing to turn off the force of psychic energy which presses to be released through the channel of genital expression.

In *some* priests and religious, especially those who have had an extremely happy and loving childhood, this genital energy unconsciously becomes *displaced* into the other two outlets for love. When this happens, that particular priest or religious is truly fortunate and blessed. His sexual drive becomes fairly easy to control, not because it is deadened by repression but because it is *sublimated* and fulfilled through charity and friendship. He fulfills his role as parent and companion in a most complete and joyful way without experiencing undue genital temptations.

Sexual temptations are not extremely strong for the person who has the gift of sublimation. He does experience them to a degree but he is able to control them without too much effort.

This is *not* a case of suppression (the conscious removal of unwanted thoughts and feelings from his awareness) nor repression (the unconscious removal of feared material from his awareness). It is not a case of becoming apathetic or listless. The *contrary* is true! He is fully alive and he is genuinely loving. His genital energy has not been simply put out of consciousness; his genital energy has been *sublimated*, displaced to outlets of love in which it is permitted to find full expression, the outlets of charity and friendship.

However, for most of us, this task of denying fulfillment to our genital sexuality is a most difficult task. For the vast majority of celibates, the genital drive is not unconsciously sublimated; it can be controlled only by the "cold turkey" struggle of *conscious self-control*.

Years ago, when it was fairly easy for us celibates to fulfill our other needs, the control of our genital sexuality didn't seem so very difficult. In those days we felt very secure in our dedicated life, felt that we were truly someone special, felt that almost everything we did had eternal meaning. We generally felt deeply appreciated and honored.

Today, however, many of us are tempted to wonder whether priesthood or religious life has any relevant meaning for our times. Quite often we experience little or no sense of prestige. There are very few feelings of appreciation. And at the same time we also have to function without the support of nourishing friendships, and do so in a culture where the control of genital expression becomes almost a superhuman feat.

These then are the basic needs of my world system: my physical needs for air and water, for food and sleep; my expressive-assertive needs to express my feelings to one who will listen and understand my need for meaning; my love needs: charity, friendship, genital fulfillment. When I *feel free* to fulfill all these needs, I am truly a self-actualized person, happy and fulfilled.

Results of Unfulfilled Needs

What happens then when these channels are blocked and my basic needs are not fulfilled? Then the effort to lead a healthy and integrated life becomes really difficult. I can get a better picture of this difficulty through the use of an illustration. If I see my body as a cylinder which is filled with pressurized gas, the gas would represent my psychic energy, my life energy, the cylinder my body and the three openings or channels at the end of the cylinder, the basic needs of my world system.

Diagram 1.

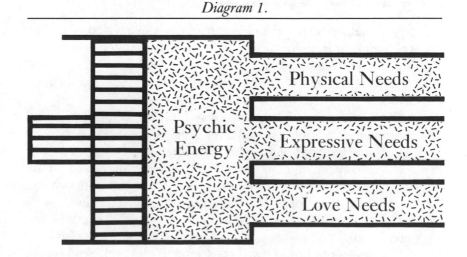

Characteristics of Psychic Energy

Note that there are two important characteristics of psychic energy. The first is that psychic energy is *energy under pressure*. It simply *has* to be discharged. If I am not free to discharge it through one or more channels, i.e., if my roadblocks and inhibitions hold me back from releasing this pressurized energy, then the pressure only continues to build up until it reaches an unmanageable pitch—and bursts out—often beyond control.

Diagram 2.

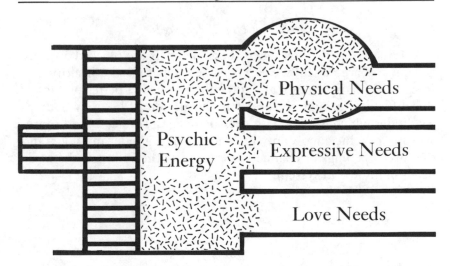

This break-out can occur either in an explosive way through its proper channel or it can be displaced to another channel.

Thus, for example, if I am deprived of food or water for a length of time, my hunger and thirst build up to such a point that I'm strongly tempted to *overeat* the first opportunity I get, or tempted to eat too fast. The energy has built up in the channel of my physical needs and bursts out explosively once it gets a chance.

This same kind of bulging phenomenon occurs when energy is *displaced* from one channel to another. Religious who can't find an outlet for their expressive needs often experience strong desires to eat too much or drink too much. And if the displaced energy goes in the direction of their love needs, they can experience an overwhelming need for affection and reassurance. At times it becomes insatiable so that no amount of affirmation seems to fill them. And when

the energy is displaced to the area of genitality, their sexual preoccupation and fantasies become almost an obsession.

There is also a third possibility. When a religious or priest is
inhibited from fulfilling his basic needs and resists all impulses for
explosive outlets, then the energy can reach such a fever pitch that
it bursts out through the walls of the cylinder itself, my body, and
causes painful psychosomatic symptoms.

Diagram 3.

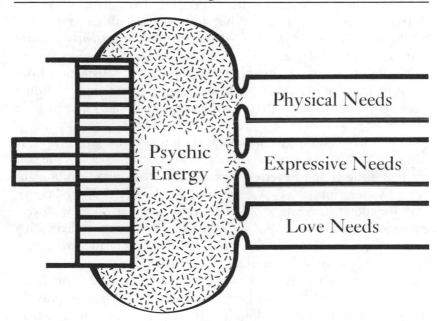

That is the second important fact about my psychic energy,
the fact that it is *fluid energy*, i.e., it is energy that can be diverted or
displaced from one channel to another. In other words, I do *not*
have a different type of energy for my physical needs than I do for
my expressive-assertive needs or for my love needs. It's all the *same
basic energy* involved in all three channels.

Psychic energy, therefore, is very similar to electrical energy.
Electricity can flow through a refrigerator and produce cold air. It
can pass through a heater and produce *hot* air, the very opposite

effect! The electrical energy itself is *fluid*. It can be converted into many different forms. Let it flow into a motor and it produces motion and power. Let it flow into power brakes and it *stops* movement. The difference in results is not due to the energy, but to the *channels* through which the energy flows!

Well, the same is true of psychic energy. It is the same life energy that is used in fulfilling all my needs: my need for food, my need for love, my need for meaning! And, because this life energy is *fluid*, it can easily be displaced to another channel when it faces any blocks or obstacles.

When only one of my basic needs is frustrated, I feel the distress of this rising pressure but I am usually able to manage a healthy adjustment, provided, of course, that I am fairly mature and have developed a fair amount of discipline and impulse control. With such maturity, I am able to find sufficient satisfaction from the fulfillment of my other needs and therefore the one unfulfilled need does not interfere with my ability to have a happy and creative life.

Thus, for example, I *am* able to give up genital satisfaction. It is not easy. There are times when this renunciation causes me real distress. One young Sister expressed her distress in a teasing manner. "I suffer a lot from C.A." she said. She had a twinkle in her eye that I couldn't understand. "You have cancer?" I asked with real concern. That's what "C.A." meant to me. "No," she replied with a knowing smile, "I suffer from *celibacy attacks*." I laughed! But I knew exactly what she meant!

However, what happens to me when *more than one* of my basic needs are not met? How do I cope with denying my genital needs, when I *also* do not have a close friend and I lack job satisfaction as well? This is not merely a theoretical question—especially for celibates who must always face life with the frustration of their genital needs as a presupposition. In all honesty we have to admit that such a situation is *not* a rare occurrence in the lives of priests and religious.

When more than one of my needs are unfulfilled, the consequences on my life can be devastating. Then the pressure of my psychic energy builds up like surging volts of electricity pouring forth from a huge generator that's "screaming" for release; like gas compressed in a cylinder by a relentless force into a smaller and smaller space. This energy, like all energy, simply *has* to be released, *has* to be discharged, either through an explosion or through displacement.

Explosive-Release

In the first possibility, the energy builds up in a channel until it reaches an explosive point and then it blasts out. Take for example the person who cannot find a listener to whom he can express his true feelings. What happens? His distress and frustration build up to such a point that he can no longer hold it in. It can then burst forth in an explosion of *compulsive talking*. Such a person goes on and on about unbelievable trivia. It is painful for anyone who is in his presence. Everyone wants to avoid him.

Unless he loses all sensitivity to those around him, he begins to sense the fact that people are pulling back and avoiding him. This only increases his isolation and frustration. Now, more than ever, he feels the need to talk. He finds himself pouring out his feelings even to strangers on a subway. In extreme cases, where all have pulled back from him because he is "strange," he finds himself alone, in his room, talking to himself.

The same process can take place in the person who has no outlet for his genital drive. Unless he exercises great self-control, the built-up pressure can come bursting out in *compulsive genitality*. He finds himself overwhelmed with sexual desires and curiosity. Almost against his will and certainly against his better judgment, he finds himself going to see x-rated movies, engaging in frequent and compulsive masturbation. Sometimes this "acting-out" even leads him into furtive and impersonal sex, either with prostitutes or in unhealthy relationships.

The great tragedy here is that such a person not only suffers the emotional pain of continued loneliness and lack of connection with meaningful persons; the real tragedy is that he also suffers *psychic pain*—a loss of self-esteem. He feels guilty. Feels unworthy. Feels inadequate as a priest or religious. Feels that he is a hypocrite and dreads the day when he will be discovered as such and unmasked! The depression and anxiety of his psychic pain are oppressive.

Something similar happens in the case of those priests and religious who do not feel appreciated as somebody special. Often they will attempt to relieve their distress by making massive attempts to get themselves appreciated. They become "workaholics," men and women who are absolutely *driven* to perform great feats. They don't feel appreciated for their personality or interior worth, so they will get themselves appreciated for what they can *accomplish*. They become truly *driven* men and women with "tunnel vision." They eat, drink and dream *work*, without giving themselves any time for their needs, especially their need for friendship.

The only advantage to overwork as a compensation is that work is much more socially acceptable than sexual acting-out or compulsive talking and infinitely more in tune with their self-esteem. So the workaholic doesn't experience the degree of psychic pain which is felt by the compulsive talker or the sexually compulsive person. Nevertheless, he has his full share of loneliness and eventually more than his share of psychosomatic illness.

Displacement

The second possible way that psychic energy can be discharged when my needs are frustrated is that the energy is *displaced to other channels*. This can be a marvelous coping mechanism in those cases where the energy is displaced to a channel that can support the extra energy, such as the channels for charity and friendship or the channel for artistic and creative work. This is called sublimation and it is the most creative and the most healthy of all our coping mechanisms.

Unfortunately, however, sublimation probably cannot be consciously willed. Sublimation is an *unconscious* mechanism by which some of our drives which are less socially acceptable are converted into noble and socially honorable outlets. It usually takes place automatically and unconsciously in those fortunate persons whose childhood was filled with love. For such persons, receiving love and giving love have become like *second nature*. And so, for them, the displacement of "unacceptable" drives to the channel of love is a relatively easy step. It "happens" without any conscious effort on their part.

Sublimation, however, is relatively rare. Perhaps this is so because not that many people have enjoyed such a completely positive and love-filled childhood. In any case, for most of us the displacement of our psychic energy tends to be not in the direction of sublimation but in the direction of the other channels, where it tends to find release in an unhealthy way.

For example, when my love needs are not met, all too often this energy is displaced to the channel of my physical needs and I develop a series of *love-substitutes*. I begin to eat too much, drink too much, sleep too much, go to the racetrack three or four times a week. Sometimes my love-substitute takes the form of getting caught up in consumerism, a passion by which I feel that I *have* to have all the latest gadgets—the best color TV, a remote-control VCR, the finest car, the best clothes, etc. Or I have to eat in the finest restaurants and attend all the best shows.

Sometimes I get caught up into hobbies that are no longer just hobbies, but all-consuming preoccupations that take me miles away from my apostolate. I become a fire buff; a police buff. One priest I know became so involved in real estate deals that to all intents and purposes he was more a real estate agent than he was a priest.

At other times when my assertive needs are frustrated, I develop *assertive-substitutes*. That is, I begin to experience an *excessive need* for understanding and affirmation. This happens all too often, and when it does I expect that everyone on every occasion should know just how I feel and be sensitive to me, or else I am terribly hurt. Sometimes I try to hide the hurt; sometimes I pout and fume like a baby.

Take Sara, for example, a dispensed Sister in her early forties who placed unbelievable demands on everyone around her. She was highly intelligent and exceptionally intuitive and sensitive. Her history was that of an emotionally deprived child. She never felt listened to or understood by either father or mother. She felt that her feelings were not accepted by them, so eventually she stopped trying to express them. She spent most of her childhood as a lonely, isolated little girl. Her companions were her books.

Her dependency needs, her needs to be a child and be loved and listened to and cared for, those needs were never adequately met. And, since nature doesn't skip any steps, she still felt those needs in adulthood. There was a constant conflict within her between her desire to be a woman and her craving to be a child. Unfortunately, it was often the persistent, angry, petulant child that dominated her interpersonal relationships.

Everyone was supposed to be keenly sensitive to her. Not only to her expressed feelings but even to those that were unexpressed. "They should know how I feel! They are *so* insensitive!" The slightest bit of hurt became magnified to a huge insult. A failure to call her at the exact time one had promised became a deliberate put-down and rejection.

She not only magnified hurts for herself but she also *identified* unconsciously with all those who were hurting and she reached out to them with very delicate care and concern. But *God help them* if they were not equally sensitive in return! She would cut them down with a tongue that was sharper than any sword! As a result most people pulled back from her—only increasing her frustration and loneliness.

Progress in counseling her was very slow because the counselor above all others was supposed to be able to listen with a hundred percent accuracy and respond with almost infinite understanding and care. As the psalmist put it: "Who is he and we shall praise him!"

Psychosomatic Illness

The third possible result, when my needs are frustrated, is that I fall a victim to psychosomatic illness. This occurs all too often in religious life and priesthood precisely because religious and priests are noble people. When a person is so strong and so nobly motivated that he or she won't use love-substitutes or assertive substitutes, what happens then? The same thing that would happen to a boiling kettle if I stopped up the spout so that the steam could not escape. The pressure inside would build up to such a point that the kettle would blow-up and burst. The built-up psychic energy bursts the cylinder and the person's body becomes the victim of psychosomatic sickness—severe headaches, high blood pressure, ulcers, unbelievable tensions.

Teresa, for example, was a physically healthy and robust young woman in her mid-thirties. A few years ago she got a position with an excellent salary but one which was extremely demanding. It was a position usually reserved for men, so she had to put up with an awful lot of teasing and harassment from her fellow workers. Besides the job itself was physically and emotionally demanding.

Teresa stuck to it doggedly, determined to prove that she could do it but the toll that all the distress took on her body was terrible. She had constant headaches, insomnia, high blood pressure and ulcer pains. Eventually she had to give up the job.

She didn't feel accepted as a person of worth. She was too tired to make any time for friends. And she was too fine a person to allow herself to *act-out* in either love-substitutes or expressive substitutes. So the pressure of her psychic energy built up to the point that the cylinder of her body began to crack beneath it.

Happiness Is Freedom

The truly healthy and happy person is the person who feels *free* and competent to fulfill all the needs of his world system. He feels free to meet his physical needs. He gets sufficient sleep, takes time for leisure and solitude, eats sensibly and well. He is free to express his feelings and careful to choose a person who is able to listen and care. He is free to seek the kind of work that he finds satisfying and enjoys doing it well. He listens to others with care and concern. He takes the risks necessary to reach out to make real friends. And he has a healthy, fulfilling sexual life in his marriage.

Stress for such a person is at a minimum. His needs are met. He doesn't suffer from psychic pain either. Experiencing himself accepted as someone special and enjoying the approbation and affection flowing from the friendships in his life, he also approves of himself and loves himself.

Built-In Tension of Celibacy

As a celibate, however, I have some built-in tensions in my world system precisely because one channel for the release of my psychic energy *has* to be partially blocked. I am not permitted to enter a genital love relationship. I may not permit myself to enjoy genital satisfaction in any way. This is a definite source of distress. No matter how eloquently spiritual writers may talk about celibacy as an eschatological sign, no matter how it may be defended as a means to make the priests and religious more available to others in their apostolate, the hard, cold fact remains that a normal channel for the release of life energy has to be blocked with all the build-up of the tensions involved in any capping of energy. For most celibates this tension in controlling their sexual drive is a source of great *distress*.

The rationale given for celibacy is a noble one, i.e., that the celibate's genital energy should be sublimated into the charity of greater apostolic work. The problem with that rationale, however, is that sublimation, as we have seen above, is *not* subject to my conscious self-control. It is an unconscious defense mechanism. Sometimes, in some fortunate people, sublimation *does* take place— and the gracious generosity which it produces in their lives and in their apostolate is beautiful.

For *most* celibates, however, sublimation does *not* take place. They have to exercise conscious self-control to hold back their genital energy. And they do so at no small price in terms of tension and fear.

Containment of Genitality

In order to live a life without genitality and to do so in a healthy way, I have to accomplish several tasks. I have to avoid suppression of my genital feelings on the one hand. Suppressing them from conscious awareness does not defuse or weaken their powerful drive. I have to keep those feelings from building up to such a pitch that they will explode in compulsive sexual acting out. And finally I have to avoid displacement of my genital energy through outlets that are destructive and self-defeating. These are not easy tasks, but neither are they impossible.

Any submersion of my genital drive, whether it is by unconscious repression or by conscious suppression, does not help. Psychic energy is still energy seeking a release whether or not I am conscious of it. Pushing it into my unconscious only means that I now have *less control* over it than I had before. Now it can seek a release in unhealthy substitutes, such as excessive eating or drinking, etc.

On the other hand, I must not let the energy build up to such a point that I begin to act out my genital drive in a compulsive way. True, I cannot consciously sublimate this energy to the service of charity or creative work. However, I *can* make myself take a *more active interest* in my apostolate. I *can* be more *available* to others with my concern and care. I *can make time* to be with my friends in wholesome recreation and affection. I can nourish an interest in good literature, art and music. I can do all this, and *then* possibly some of the genital energy will be drained off slowly and gradually into these wholesome outlets. I cannot *force* that to happen but I can encourage it, and very often this wholesome strategy is successful.

Finally, I must make sure that all my other channels for the release of psychic energy are wide open, i.e., all the others besides the channel for genital expression. I must see to it that my physical needs are met through a healthy diet, sufficient exercise and recreation, sufficient sleep and some necessary leisure in privacy and solitude. I must not let myself think of these outlets as *luxuries* that I could put aside at any time without harm.

I must also make sure that my expressive-assertive needs are met. I have to find someone, friend or counselor, to whom I can pour out my feelings. And if I am not appreciated as someone special in my work situation, I must take the necessary steps either to make myself appreciated there or find appreciation and respect in another area of work.

And finally, I must reach out to others with love. I must experience myself as an actively caring and sensitive person. And, above all, I need to experience the love of friends who genuinely like me and enjoy my company.

When all these channels are open, then the conscious control of my genital drive becomes possible and bearable.

Vocation Crisis

One final point: the fact that celibacy is a possible life style does not necessarily make mandatory celibacy a *desirable* discipline. The Church seems to be paying a terribly high price for making celibacy a necessary condition for ordination. Whatever value celibacy has as a *sign* seems to be far outweighed by the negative effects it has had in discouraging vocations.

It isn't only the loss of active personnel! That is tragic enough, considering that we have lost thousands of excellent apostolic priests from the active ministry. (Of the hundreds of resigned priests whom I have met or worked with, all but a few who left did so in order to get married.) Most people are aware of these losses.

What may not be so apparent is the number who have taken

their conflict *underground* by using *love-substitutes*. Some have sought a solution for their loneliness in alcohol; others seek comfort at the race track or in consumerism; some seek relief in sexual acting-out. The latter especially experience intense shame as well as cause scandal.

Some very sincere men handle their loneliness by overwork. There is less psychic pain for workaholics, but eventually, too, they pay a high price in psychosomatic illness and/or burnout. Perhaps the saddest of all are those who become apathetic—men whose psychic pain has reached such an intensity that they have turned off *all* feelings both of pain and joy. They have no enthusiasm, no sparkle or luster. They exist but they are not alive.

One cannot help but wonder whether *any* discipline which seems so self-defeating can truly be called a *sign* of His Kingdom.

Conclusion

Fulfilling my world needs, then, is a big step on the road to achieving happiness and a life free of distress and pain. *Genuine freedom* is this freedom to live life fully, to live with the serenity and joy that comes when my needs are fulfilled.

Most of us do not experience this freedom. Sometimes the roadblocks come *from without*. I long for someone in my life to whom I can pour out my feelings, someone who will accept me and love me as I am, and too often, no one is there and I feel frustrated and distressed.

Most often, however, the roadblocks are *from within*, from my own inhibitions and fears which hold me back and refuse me the "permission" to fulfill my outer needs.

How can I get past these internal roadblocks and allow myself the freedom to live, to live fully? The answer to that lies with another psychic system, my self-system. As strange as it may seem at first sight, the truth is that almost all success or failure in fulfilling my *outer* needs depends upon my success or failure in fulfilling my *inner* needs. Psychic pain, low self-esteem, is the *most inhibiting roadblock* of all. How I feel about myself is the essential ingredient in how I achieve in my outer world.

CHAPTER III

My Self System

Overview

My person, like my body, is made up of several systems which interact with one another and depend on one another. In my body, for example, I have a bone system, which is like the structural steel in a building. Without my skeleton, I'd be only a big blob of protoplasm—unable to stand erect or move. And yet, my bones do not form an independent system, because they cannot move by themselves. They need the muscle system, which pulls them in the direction in which I want them to move.

But my muscles are not independent either. They cannot contract by themselves. The muscles need the fuel supply which is given by my blood system and they need an ignition spark which is supplied by my brain and my nervous system. And, of course, the blood system also is not independent. The blood wouldn't have any fuel or air to give unless it received it from the digestive system and the respiratory system.

In my body then these systems *interact* upon each other and are *dependent* on each other. Consequently, a major breakdown in any system causes drastic effects on all the other systems. A blood clot in the brain, for example, can cut off oxygen to the brain and cause death which is the collapse of all the systems.

Well, the same is true in my psychic life—my person. As I see it, I have *three psychic systems*, which interact upon one another so intimately and depend on one another so closely that a breakdown in any system can cause terrible damage in the other systems. So, as we saw in the last chapter, I have:

1. *My world-system*—the way in which I relate to my outer world. I am immersed in a world of people and things. I have a unique contribution that I need to make to my world. And I have very definite needs which have to be fulfilled by that world. When I fail here, the resulting damage is not only to my body but to my psyche as well. I experience the psychic pain of a diminished self-esteem.

2. *My self-system*—This is the way in which I relate to myself and the way that I feel about myself. My greatest joys and my severest pains are felt in this system. When I fail to achieve a healthy self-esteem, I not only experience psychic pain but I also feel inhibited from fulfilling the needs of my world system. The two systems interact upon one another.

3. Finally, I have *my perceptive-system*—the way in which I perceive and interpret the realities in my other two worlds. This system, as we shall see, is the most important of all.

How much these systems depend on each other will become more clear as we study the second and third systems in detail.

Self-System

Let's look now at this second system, my self-system. The importance of this system cannot be exaggerated because practically all success in fulfilling my outer needs depends upon my degree of success in my self-system. Why? Because it is here in my inner world that I achieve the joy and freedom to become my complete self. And it is here also that I mostly suffer emptiness and inhibition and despair.

No other feeling can possibly substitute for the way that I feel about myself. No achievement in my outer world can bring me happiness if I don't feel happy about myself. Even having a tremendous job and prestige, great physical beauty, even a huge amount of respect and love from those around me! All of these can fail to touch me, can leave me empty and depressed, if I look down upon myself and despise myself.

So, if my world-system is my Holy Place, in which I seek fulfillment and satisfaction, and it is, then my self-system is my very Holy of Holies—my inner sanctuary. Either I "make it" here in my self-system, or I'm simply a washout in life! My self-system means as much to my person as blood means to my body!

My self-system may be defined as a way in which I relate to myself and the way I feel about myself. This system is healthy and vibrant when I feel a strong sense of self-esteem; when I see clearly who I am and I am delighted at what I see!

Actually, this beautiful vision of self is the fullness of the virtue of humility. Humility is not only the cornerstone of the spiritual life; it is the cornerstone of psychological health as well. Why? Precisely because humility is honesty. It means that I have a clear knowledge of who I am plus a joyful, wholehearted contentment to be just that.

Self-Esteem
Parents' Greatest Gift to Their Children

If I am fortunate, this beautiful vision of myself is bestowed upon me in early childhood and enriches my entire life forever after. My parents have the power to define me, so to speak, the power to tell me who I am and what I am, in a word, the power to tell me whether I am truly worthwhile or just mediocre or of no real worth at all.

When I am born, I have absolutely no idea who I am or what I am worth—no more than I can know what I look like without a mirror to reflect my image back to me. Well, my parents are the mirror of my personality and worth. How they respond to me, warm and loving, or cold and rejecting, determines just how I see myself. I am truly fortunate if the message they give me is that I am of inestimable value.

A recent example of this was the experiment conducted by Dr. Edgar Rey at San Juan de Dios Hospital in Bogotá, Colombia. Dr. Rey had observed that all the premature babies who were less than 2.2 pounds died, no matter how carefully they were cared for in the incubators. So he directed that all the babies under 2.2 pounds be put immediately next to their mother's breast inside her hospital gown and remain there for a few weeks. The results were startling. Seventy-five percent of these babies now lived. They were held closely by mother; they felt wanted, cherished, warm. They could feed from their mother's breast whenever they wanted to; there were no set intervals for bottles. The warmth, the closeness, the constant giving by mother demonstrated better than any mirror that they were *wanted* and *lovable* and supremely worthwhile! And that was enough to pull seventy-five percent of them through the dangerous first few weeks.

If I am *not* so fortunate in childhood, the lack of this beautiful vision of myself can impoverish me for as long as I live. Early childhood is the proper time to achieve self-esteem, when the cement of my personality is still soft and impressionable. If I do not achieve it at that time, if instead of self-love, self-hatred is imprinted on the soft cement of my psyche, then once that cement hardens it is extremely difficult to change what has been written. It is *not impossible* to change it! We are the *products* of our childhood; we are not the prisoners! We can change! We can grow!

Some time ago a minister asked one of the young boys in his parish, "Who made you, son?" The boy thought for a moment, wrinkled his brow and answered: "To tell you the truth, sir, I'm not finished!" That is the truth of the matter! As long as we live, we are "not yet finished." We can change. But it is extremely difficult. We will consider this more in detail later on. For the present, let's consider the basic elements of self-esteem.

The Basic Elements of My Self-Esteem

There are three basic elements which make up a healthy sense of self-esteem. These are the three *needs* of my internal world. *All three* must be fulfilled if my feelings about myself are to be positive and healthy.

1. I must feel that I am *good*, i.e., I must see myself as noble, attractive, lovable; attractive in the deep sense of this word.

   The opposite of this healthy feeling is the feeling of neurotic guilt or shame—the awful feeling that I am ugly or bad, not lovable. This feeling is really neurotic because it is not true! None of us are really ugly or bad. That is what the Gospel message is all about! "God so loved the world that He sent His Son" —*God* loves us! God, Who sees all things as they really are! God Who measures all things by a true yardstick of values! But *I* have to know that! *I* have to *feel* that!

2. Secondly, I must feel that I'm *intelligent*, i.e., I must feel that I have talent, that I'm capable and adequate for the work that I have to do, adequate for my situation in life. I need to feel that I have the ability to cope and manage.

Martha, a Sister in her mid-forties, was put in charge of the home for the senior Sisters of her community because of her beautiful qualities of sensitivity and thoughtfulness. The entire Council approved of her appointment and the older Sisters were most pleased with her.

She felt a conflict, however, between herself and a member of the Council who was in charge of retirement. And when it came to a showdown on whose opinion would be honored, she felt that the Provincial always supported the Council member instead of herself. This hurt her no end and diminished her feelings for herself. In spite of all the reassurance she received from the Provincial, in spite of the fact that the Sisters she cared for spoke of her as a good and compassionate woman, she was not able to feel good about herself because she did not feel that they respected her as an *intelligent* woman. "I'm sick of them telling me how good I am," she complained. "I want them to respect my intelligence!" I understood how she felt. Each of us needs to feel that we are intelligent and adequate.

The opposite of this feeling is a neurotic inferiority complex. Again, I say "neurotic" because in actuality no one is inferior for his or her work in life. I can *feel* inferior when others ridicule me or put me down, or when I set up impossible goals for myself and then excoriate myself for not achieving them. But these feelings are inappropriate. They do not reflect the reality.

I can also *feel* inferior when I make the mistake of comparing myself with others. Others are meant for a different work in life and, therefore, have different talents than I have. So, comparisons are always wrong and always destructive! When I compare myself to others, I either end up looking down on them, which makes me insufferably stuffy and proud; or, what is worse, I end up looking down on myself with all the consequent depression and anxiety of psychic pain.

3. Thirdly, I must feel that I have power, i.e., I must feel that I am endowed with *interior power*. By this I do not mean physical strength but rather that interior moral power by which I am able to *lead my own life* and make my own decisions, the power to pull my own strings.

The opposite to this is the neurotic feeling of helplessness, the feeling of being trapped. Again, I use the word "neurotic" in connection with this feeling of helplessness because in reality I am not helpless! None of us is helpless! We each have the *right* and the *power* to live our own life.

I can *feel* helpless when I give away that power, when I strive so hard to live up to what *others* expect of me rather than what *I* know I should be. Then I feel trapped! But I am not helpless in reality. Even after I have given away my power to others and allow them to dominate my life, even then I am not helpless because I always have the ability to take that power back!

Henry, for example, felt trapped every Sunday because he felt that he *had* to go to his mother-in- law's for Sunday dinner. He resented it terribly. For him it was worse than going to work. He couldn't see the football game. He had to listen to the same old stories from his father-in-law. He hated going! But he saw no way to get out of it. Each time he tried to refuse, his wife would nag him and make him feel selfish. So he gave in every week and hated himself for being so weak.

He *felt* trapped but in reality he was not helpless. And with some counseling he was able to take back the power over his life. One day he said to his wife: "Mary, I'm not going to your mother's this afternoon. I don't like the feeling that I've had all these years. I've felt manipulated and trapped. *You* go and explain that I'll come occasionally but I need some time for myself." There was some fuss but he stuck to his guns, and he felt like a new person!

These are the three essential elements of self-esteem, the three needs, so to speak, of my internal world. It is from fulfilling *all* these needs that I achieve a healthy self-esteem. When I have achieved all three, then my greatest need in life has been met, because now I feel tremendous about myself. I'm on top of the world! And the task of fulfilling my other needs, the needs of my world-system, that task becomes a pushover because now I am truly free!

I make sure that I get enough food and maintain a balanced diet. I get enough sleep and enough exercise. I make sure that I don't put on too much weight. I have too much self-respect to allow that to happen! It is *easy* now to be good to myself, because now I love myself. I dress neatly and professionally. I reflect in my appearance my own good inner feelings.

Some years ago in a group at the Center one of the sisters came to the group dressed in a way that could only be described as slovenly. Her hair wasn't combed and she wore sloppy jeans and a worn and unkempt blouse. The way she looked reflected exactly the way she felt about herself. After interacting for two or three months in the group, however, during which time she expressed her painful feelings and received exceptionally warm and positive feedback from the other members of the group, she began to dress in an entirely different manner. She was neat, well-groomed and wore a very attractive jumper and blouse. Several of the religious and priests in the group remarked to her: "Wow, Susan, do you look different!" Her new appearance was just the outward reflection of her feelings of esteem about herself.

When I have self-esteem, I can also fulfill my expressive needs and my assertive needs. I can share my feelings with trusted friends. Why is it so easy for me now? Because I feel so good about myself, I also feel great about my feelings. I'm in no way ashamed of them! I feel *alive* because of them! So it is easy for me to share them and to share them clearly and with appropriate effect, so that my friends know exactly how I feel. I can also *respond* with open and honest feeling to what others say to me. I'm real, unaffected, genuine. There is no need for me to put on an act. I *know* that I'm okay!

When I like myself, I am also able to get a satisfying job. I'm able to choose an apostolate that fits my temperament and talents. I can even relate beautifully with Jesus and really believe that He loves me! I have a happy, bright outlook on life that is absolutely contagious.

And most of all, I can make the gift of myself to others in real love. Because I feel great about myself, I am not constantly preoccupied with my own problems or constantly wondering how other people feel about me. Because *I* feel good about me, I just presuppose that *you* feel good about me also. I project my own good feelings about myself onto you, and I feel that you also love and respect me. So it is very easy for me now to like you. It's easy for me to be present to you, to be pre-occupied with your problems and your feelings. And, of course, those warm and positive signals on my part make *me* very attractive in your eyes, and so you respond warmly to me. A good relationship is easily established between us.

Self-love, then, a healthy self-esteem, is the master key by which I can unlock all the valves in my world-system and meet all the needs I have in relation to the world about me. And, as those needs are met, they only tend to *reinforce* the good feelings about myself that I already have. It's no wonder that Jesus said, "To those who have, more will be given!" "The kingdom of God is truly within us," within our self-system.

My Strongest Defenses Are Those Protecting My Self-System

Now, since this is true, since my self-esteem is my most treasured possession and the key by which I unlock all the valves in my world-system, then naturally it follows that I erect my *strongest defenses* to protect this feeling about myself.

My most sensitive radar, my most elaborate psychic computers, my most complete line of defense mechanisms—are all drawn up in constant alert to ward off any threat to my self-esteem.

When my self-esteem is fairly well-grounded, I defend myself in a firm but moderate way. I am able to listen to your criticism, evaluate what might be true and distinguish what is true from what is exaggerated and false. I use the true criticism to become a better person. I discard the rest. Because my self-esteem is healthy, my defenses are realistic and moderate. When my sense of self is shaky or poor, however, then my defenses are immoderate and often aggressive.

And so, for example, I am extremely sensitive to the *slightest hint* you make that I may not be good, that I may not be smart, not self-directed. The moment I become aware of such a suggestion, I become terribly defensive, almost to the point of not hearing what you are saying.

If you accuse me of being jealous, for example, I'll probably start denying it before you even finish your sentence. "How *dare* you make such an insinuation! Who do you think you are, playing psychologist!" I don't even let the *possibility* of my being jealous come anywhere near me.

Or, if you put me down, ridicule me, make me look stupid, and regretfully this happens all too often even in community life, immediately I'll fight like a tiger to change that impression. I'll attack you! I'll tell you that you don't know what the hell you are talking about! I just feel that I *have* to counteract that impression at all costs because if I begin to believe that I *am* stupid, I suffer the awful pain of looking down on myself.

It's almost unbelievable to what lengths I will go in order to feel better about myself. For example, Edward, a priest in his late thirties, was persuaded to come in for counseling because he loved to do things that were not only bizarre for a priest, but also very dangerous. He would dress in a leather jacket and ride his motorcycle at breakneck speeds on highways and dirt roads and up steep hills. Often he would ride into Harlem, get off the motorcycle and swagger into a bar where he would exude an attitude of "devil-may-care."

Friends who cared about him tried to reason with him to be more prudent. To no avail! He'd say, "I don't know why but I get such a 'high' when I do things like this. I just feel so great!" Finally his friends succeeded in persuading him to come for counseling. They managed this with some help from his deep depression which he often experienced between his escapades.

Edward's history revealed a childhood in which he was constantly over-protected by an anxiety-ridden mother. He was never allowed to participate in sports. He might get hurt. She wrote notes to the school to keep him from taking part in the gym classes. In cold weather he was always over-dressed so he wouldn't catch cold. The other children were cruel. They called him a "sissy" and treated him as a weakling. His own image of himself was that he was inferior as a boy and inferior as a man.

It soon became clear that all his "dare-devil" escapades were mainly an attempt to prove to himself that this awful image was wrong. Far from being unmanly, he was the very exemplar of courage and daring. Just look at his fearlessness! He seemed willing to take *any risk* in order to feel better about himself.

If space permitted it would be fascinating to treat in great detail the unbelievable lengths to which we will go in order to protect our self-esteem or to enhance it. We will not only use *avoiding* defenses in order to run away from psychic pain, defenses like denial, repression and rationalization, but we will also use *attacking* defenses like sarcasm, ridicule, abrasiveness and projection—all to throw the pain back onto the other person, to pretend that it is the other person's problem not ours! He's the one who should feel badly about himself—not I!

Sister Mary, for example, read a great many romantic novels but couldn't get herself to admit that she was curious about sexual matters. She was a religious with a vow of chastity. How could she be interested in the sexual escapades detailed in a novel!

She couldn't reconcile such curiosity with her image of what a good religious should be. It was too painful for her to *own* curiosity. So she used rationalization. It wasn't for herself that she read the novels. Personally she found them very offensive! Her only purpose in reading them was to understand better what her students were reading. It was really a noble thing she was doing because she was putting herself through a lot of distress just to be able to understand and help others.

It was sad that she could not *own* her curiosity and realize that curiosity about sex did not make her a bad person. It only showed that she was human! The point here, however, is that above all else she had to defend herself against a lessening of self-esteem. And to do that she used denial and rationalization.

We will not only use all the defenses we can to protect ourselves against a poor self-image, but we will also make great sacrifices in order to *increase* our self-image. To feel a little more attractive, for example, we will undergo the pains, the risks and the expense of plastic surgery. Many of us practically "kill ourselves" dieting and exercising just to feel a little more slim and attractive. Women will pay a lot of money and go through real pain to have hair removed from their face. Men will do the same thing to have hair implanted on their head.

Self-Esteem—The Core of Happiness

I am not saying that these extraordinary efforts on our part are bad things to do! What I am saying is that such efforts demonstrate very clearly that self-esteem is the *very core* of real happiness. We prize it so highly that we will do *almost anything* to gain it, anything to protect it.

Whether we are conscious of it or not, self-esteem is the central source of joy behind almost every other joy— and the lack of it is the central source of pain behind most other pains.

For example, the happiness which I feel when you show me that you love me is not mainly the joy that *you* love me. True, your love does mean a lot to me and part of my joy flows from embracing your care and admiration. However, what touches me *most deeply* about your loving me is the fact that *I can now love myself*! Now I can feel that I am lovable! You love me, so that tells me that I am good and attractive and a person of great worth! And the feeling is exhilarating.

Why is this feeling about myself so important? Because as close as you may be to me, I am more close to myself. So, while your loving me warms me, *my* loving me, *my* feeling that I am beautiful and good, that just thrills me!

Conversely, when you reject me, the *deepest hurt* I feel is not the loss of your friendship. That loss does hurt, of course, and it hurts a lot, because you are dear to me! But the deepest pain for me is the ugly feeling which I now have about *myself*. Because you have rejected me, I now feel that I must be unattractive, unlovable. I feel that I must be ugly. And that is about the worst feeling that I can have.

It is this fear of psychic pain that holds back so many religious and priests from ever achieving deep friendships in their lives. They absolutely *dread* rejection because of how it makes them feel about themselves. Most of them have felt this great pain earlier in their lives and they never want to experience anything like it again. So, as much as they hunger for the comfort and support of close

friends, they pull back from closeness because they perceive closeness as a deceptive trap—"sweet to the lips but bitter to the taste."
Let themselves value someone that much and they automatically
give that person the power to scald them by withdrawal and rejection. It's too great a risk, they conclude! Consciously or unconsciously they decide that it is not worth the risk! So they ward off
rejection by warding off closeness. How sad! They remain awfully
lonely. They have no one who really knows them or deeply cares!

Such priests and religious are often very zealous and apostolic.
They give of themselves constantly. They are cheerful, kind,
thoughtful. If a member of your family dies, they are present at the
wake and funeral Mass. They send you a Mass Card. They write
the most moving letters of sympathy and concern. If there is anything that they can do, be sure to let them know, they'd be only too
happy to help!

Do you need someone to take your turn at duty? Never hesi-
tate to ask. They are glad to take it for you. Need someone to help
you put away the groceries? They are there without your even
asking. Someone to drive you to the dentist and wait for you?
Absolutely! No trouble at all. Glad to do it!

But—don't misinterpret these signals. They are *not* invitations
to closeness! Far from it. They are "bribes" that are offered to take
the place of closeness. When other less fearful people do things like
this for you, it is usually a sign that they would like to have a closer
relationship with you. Their acts of kindness are outward signs by
which they say, "Look, this is how much I care about you! I'd love
to be closer to you!"

But that is far from the case for the fearful people. Instead of
their actions saying, "This is proof of how much I care for you,"
their acts of love say: "Take these acts of kindness *instead* of my
getting close to you! I want you to feel my sympathy for your pain.
I want you to know that I'm concerned about you. It will please me
no end if what I do for you makes you feel better about yourself.
But please don't ask me to share *myself* with you because closeness
terrifies me! Rejection always follows it, and I simply cannot bear
that pain!"

That scalding pain, which they dread so much, is not just the
loss of a friendship, the discomfort of the distancing from a former
loved one. The *core* of that burning pain is the loss of self-esteem

which the rejection causes. "I'm rejected, so I must be worthless. I'm no longer cherished, so I simply must not be attractive or lovable." The very core of their fear of closeness, the moving force behind their signals of "Don't come near," is their dread of feeling worse about themselves.

Joanne, for example, a delightful young woman of nineteen, had come for counseling to cope with her painful feelings of un-requited love. She was "crazy" about one of the young men in her circle of friends but he hardly seemed to notice her. After a few months in counseling and some input on taking the risk to give clearer signals about her feelings, she apparently attracted his atten-tion. One day she came to the rectory "floating on air" with happi-ness. I thought that I'd have to pull her down from the ceiling! The young man she liked not only noticed her but asked her to be his steady girl friend. I felt so good for her.

It is hard to believe at first, however, how she then handled his invitations for dates. She never accepted a single date! Each time he called, she would say to her mother, "Tell him that I'm out! Tell him that I'm sick!" It was so sad. After five or six attempts, he finally gave up calling.

The tragic part of all this was that she desired love fiercely and would have reciprocated his love beautifully. *But*, she feared that once he really got to know her, he would be displeased with her, find her inadequate and eventually reject her. And that fear was so overpowering that she couldn't let herself take the chance. It was so ironic. Her fear accomplished the very rejection that she dreaded!

In my twenty years of counseling at the Center, I experienced untold hundreds of splendid, dedicated priests and religious who lived with loneliness all the time, without understanding or the emotional support of dear friends. They were *tied up* by their fears, either the fear of rejection or the fear of loss of control, both of which would have been intolerable for their self-esteem.

These priests and religious were masters at *giving love*. They were charitable, kind, generous in their ministry, many times even to an excess. But they didn't *receive* love. They didn't experience the comfort of others giving to them. They hungered for love, but they also dreaded love. Consciously or unconsciously, they felt that their shaky self-esteem just couldn't take one more blow. The tragic part, of course, was that an experience of emotional love was *precisely* the experience they needed in order to re-build their weakened self-esteem. Their defense against closeness kept them from the very refreshment they needed most.

The same defense of my self-concept underlies my longing for success and self-direction as well as my dread of failure and my dread of feeling trapped.

My achieving success and enjoying the praise and recognition which it brings is a very pleasant experience. Praise and honor are most enjoyable. I recognize that very easily. What I don't always advert to in a conscious way is that the core of that joy is the nice feeling that I now can feel about myself. "I've been honored—so I must be adequate. I must be smart." That's the nicest feeling of all! I value it highly when *you* think that I am smart but when *I* feel it, it warms me in my innermost being.

And, of course, the very opposite is true when I fail in a project or fail in my examinations. The disappointment at not succeeding is nowhere near as painful as the haunting voice inside me now which says that I really must be *stupid* or else I would have succeeded.

In fairness to the truth, it must be said that this is not always and absolutely true of every person! Those fortunate and rare human beings, whose parents have endowed them with a solid and unshakable self-esteem, might not suffer any significant psychic pain from rejection or failure. They feel so completely convinced of their own worth and lovableness that they are able to bear these pains without the failure or the rejection causing them to doubt themselves.

However, there are not too many people who have been so blessed. I think that most of us suffer sharp twinges of psychic pain under these circumstances, and it is *this* pain that hurts us the most. And it is the *dread* of feeling this psychic pain that makes us most defensive and belligerent when facing criticism or correction.

Conclusion

Two very important conclusions follow from this. The first is that one of the cruelest things that I can ever do to another person is to cause him psychic pain by diminishing his self-esteem. Other pains cut at his body or his feelings. Psychic pain cuts at his very heart.

Just as no other happy feeling can quite equal the exhilaration of feeling great about myself, so no other pain is quite so all-embracing and debilitating as self-hatred. Even those physical pains, which are certainly terribly hard to bear, are not quite so devastating in their effects on my personality as psychic pain. For once I lack self-esteem, all my other resources become diminished and ineffective.

And yet it is tragic how often this kind of cruelty takes place—even among priests and religious. Much of it is not conscious—at least we are not fully aware of the far-reaching consequences of our words and actions, but the *damage* is just as great as if we did know. Everytime I fail to be sensitive to your feelings, I communicate to you the message that you are not too important. Everytime I pull back from you, even though I do so because of my own fears of closeness, you feel rejected. You don't realize that it is *my* problem. You feel that it is *your* problem—that you are not lovable or worthwhile!

And then when I consider those ugly things that I can sometimes do or say when I'm in a bad mood, those ways that I can tear you down or cut you to shreds by my sarcasm and ridicule, those behaviors are cruel beyond measure because they make you feel like dirt! I tell you that you are stupid. I mock you for the way you walk or talk or laugh. I ridicule your mannerisms. I laugh at your opinions. I call others to witness the "stupidity" of your remarks! Lord, what cruelty that is! You are *devasted*! —humiliated beyond words! You reel in agony because your sense of self has been ripped from you. It would be less cruel if I took a knife and slashed your face!

It is cruel beyond words to describe when I do anything or say anything that makes you feel put-down or inadequate. Anything that implies that you are stupid or ugly or bad. I not only hurt your body when I do that: not only wound your feelings, I cut you in the very depths of your personality. I strike at your personhood! I cause you such pain that you are all but rendered immobile to recover your equilibrium.

And yet that kind of cruelty is widespread—leaving broken, bleeding, hurting persons in its path. People will mock others for being short or fat or bald. They will call attention to a misformed nose or a turned eye or a crippled limb. They will put others down because of their race or lack of education or for mispronounciations in their speech. Most times this is done, I'm sure, without the offender having the slightest realization of the penetrating pain he is causing or the long-lasting injury to the other person's self-esteem.

Helen, for example, a young Sister in her late thirties, lived with chronic depression. She felt unattractive because of a slightly protruding upper lip, even though in reality she was quite pretty.

Her low estimate of herself began when she was a young girl. A group of boys from her class laughed at her and called her "dog-face!" That was absolutely devastating for her. The pain of it still brought tears to her eyes after all those years. Her perception of herself had been terribly damaged and all because of an insensitive and cruel put-down.

Probably each one of us knows people who have been scarred in similar ways by being called "fatty," "stupid," "ugly," "a fag." Now they perceive themselves through this distorting filter and they can hardly see their true beauty at all!

There's such a need, especially for priests and religious, to raise their consciousness in this regard. No blow is so painful and far-reaching as a blow to a person's self-esteem. Insensitivity to psychic pain over-shadows all other cruelties.

Affirmation—The Most Beautiful Gift

The second conclusion, conversely, is that the most beautiful gift that I can give to another is to *enhance* his self-esteem by sensitivity and affirmation. When I do that, I truly give him, in a very effective way, the *gift of himself*. I give him a new sense of himself, a new insight into his beauty and goodness, a new appreciation and joy in himself, a new confidence that radiates throughout his whole personality. I give him the key whereby he is able to unlock all the treasures of his world system and fulfill all his needs. He is able to be sure that his affective needs and assertive needs are fulfilled. And, above all, because he now feels in his innermost core that he is beautiful and lovable, he has no hesitation about making the gift of himself in love. My sensitivity and affirmation have called him forth to life. In a very real way I have *redeemed* him by my love the way Jesus redeemed me by His!

Arthur, a retired man in his fifties, led an extremely lonely life. The victim of severe scrupulosity all his life, he never let anyone get close to him. He could not trust himself to love. He would only drag other people down with him. They would end up as "bad" as he was.

In counseling, all efforts at easing his obsessive-compulsive perfectionism and merciless self-blame had only slight results, until he finally consented to be part of a self-actualizing group. One of the other members of the group was a very sensitive and compassionate woman. She had a delightful sense of humor which she always used for gentle teasing and affirmation. She got to appreciate Arthur's pain and to see his genuine goodness as a person. Appreciation soon turned into love—and in the gentlest and unhurried and most sensitive way, she communicated that to Arthur.

He resisted at first. It was just too good to believe! What could such a lovely woman possibly see in him! There was no pressure. She was just there—understanding, caring, showing by her smiles and response that she thoroughly enjoyed him.

And then gradually the iceberg that was Arthur began to melt. He ventured to take her for coffee after group. And then to dinner. And then on regular dates.

The change in him was remarkable. So much of his tension was eased. Most of his scruples faded into the distance. He began to laugh and smile and joke and tease. Arthur had been given not only the gift of a beautiful woman's love; Arthur had been given the gift of himself.

Nature of Affirmation

Affirmation or affection is the outward sign of love. Love itself is the work of my mind and my heart. In my mind I perceive your goodness and beauty. In my heart I feel a warm response to that beauty. I like you. I like being near you and talking to you. I want to know you better and I want you to know me and like me.

All these thoughts and feelings, however, remain inside of me. *You* cannot see them or feel them. They do you absolutely no good unless I show them to you by some outward signs. Well, that's exactly what affection and affirmation are! They are the *outward signs* of my appreciation and admiration—the outward signs of my love.

When I show you affirmation and affection, I not only invite you into a closer relationship with myself, but I hold up a mirror to you in which you are able to see and appreciate your own beauty and great worth. You cannot see what your face looks like without the help of a mirror. Likewise, you cannot fully appreciate your own superior goodness and loveliness until you see that loveliness reflected in the eyes and affection of someone who loves you.

What a blessed thing affection is then! And how careful we must be never to neglect showing it to the people that we appreciate and love. By it we increase their self-esteem, enliven their powers to reach out and live. We give to them the gift of their very best self.

Sensitivity

We can also enhance another's self-esteem when we are sensitive to the psychic pain which they feel and reach out to relieve it.

When I make an effort to be sensitive by putting myself, at least for the moment, in the other person's shoes, I can easily perceive the psychic pain he experiences when he is put-down or ridiculed or laughed at. Those vicious attacks upon his self-system certainly diminish his sense of self and make him feel ugly and stupid.

I may not be able to shield him from these cruel attacks. Nevertheless, I can help him no end just by letting him know that I understand what he is feeling and feel it with him. "Wow, that must have hurt so much! I'm awfully sorry!" Just that can make a tremendous difference!

And if we know him well enough to affirm him, our sensitivity and affirmation can do even more. "How sad that they have no appreciation of your wealth of knowledge or your kindness to people! I wish they knew you the way I do!" If the wounded person can hear, he may still regret the cruelty and the insensitivity of those who hurt him, but now his worst pain has been eased. He can feel good about himself again because he sees his own goodness reflected in my kindness.

This kind of sensitivity is especially loving and redemptive when I sense a person's psychic pain in those situations where it is *not* so obvious. For example, John, a religious Brother, felt very depressed because he was not appointed the Principal, as everyone had expected he would be. There were many pains he was feeling;

his embarrassment in facing everyone's quizzical "How come?"; his discomfort in feeling that somehow he had let his family down; his frustration because he felt that he could have filled the position with greater skill than the one who was appointed. All of these feelings were painful. I sensed, however, that his deepest hurt was his inner feeling that somehow he must be incapable and inadequate, that somehow he just didn't measure up.

I felt very much for this psychic pain. I listened carefully as he expressed all his conscious feelings of disappointment. I understood that this was rough, I told him. In my eyes his worth as a Brother and educator in no way depended upon the role he played in school or the job he had. His worth was in himself—in what his personality brought to the other members of the faculty and to the students who loved him dearly. I let him know that I wished that the school had more men like him on the faculty. I said all this because I really felt it. After a while, he was able to see it too and appreciate himself as much as I appreciated him.

Summary

To sum up, then, my self-system, the feeling I have about myself, is the very center of my psychic life. Happiness in life is achieved or lost right here. If I have self-esteem, I can conquer the world. I can achieve and I can enjoy my achievements. I can love and I can *believe* that I am loved in return. I can let myself be nourished by your love. And I can love God and believe that God really loves me. I am at peace!

On the other hand, if I don't have self-esteem, I can't punch my way out of a paper bag! Even the talents and achievements that I do have leave me absolutely flat and blah! I can't reach out to you and love you. I can't begin to believe that you love me. It's hard for me to believe that I am even loved by God. And I just can't forgive myself for any of my faults. I just keep blaming myself again and again.

A typical example of this unrelenting refusal to forgive self was Conrad, a priest in his early fifties. Conrad had been an ideal priest for the first twenty-two years of his priesthood; a little tense and scrupulous but extremely kind to people and very generous in his service to them.

Then in one assignment which was a lonely post, he fell in love with a woman and got sexually involved with her. He asked for a transfer and was granted one, but for years later he could not forgive himself for his "unfaithfulness." He was terribly depressed. He spoke of himself constantly in a disparaging manner. And sadly, he acted-out his depressed feelings in his work. He did everything a priest should do, but without joy or enthusiasm, without any conviction that his priestly work had any worth for others.

The other priests and religious in his group at the Center appreciated his goodness and his sorrow, but it seemed almost impossible to get him to appreciate it, or even to see it. Only after years of counseling did he begin to get a new experience of himself.

I must make myself conscious of the damages I can cause to others when I am insensitive. I hurt others unmercifully when I put them down or laugh at them or pull back from them—precisely because my cruelty goes straight to the heart of their self-esteem. And I help others most beautifully when I'm sensitive to them and affirm them. I give them joy in being who they are. I give them the gift of their true self.

What can I do to achieve self-esteem for *myself*? That's a more difficult question. The answer to it lies with another system—my perceptive system.

CHAPTER IV

My Perceptive System

Feelings Follow Perceptions

It is evident from all that has been said up to this point, that self-esteem is the key which sets me free, free to unlock all the treasures in my world system; the key to healthy self-expression, to job satisfaction, the key above all to deep and meaningful love relationships in my life.

It is also a fact that each and every person should have a beautiful self-esteem because God made each one of us beautiful and adequate for our work in life. And God gave each of us the power and the right to direct our own life. I have the *power* to pull my own strings, to be inner-directed and free. And no one has the right to deprive me of that freedom! So objectively speaking, each one of us should feel great about himself.

With a little reflection, however, I soon become aware that I and perhaps most other people suffer in varying degrees from a rather poor self-image. Far from feeling great about ourselves, so many of us feel disappointed with ourselves. Why? In reality we have so much. Why do we feel that we have so little?

The answer to that question lies within my third system, my perceptive system. The unfortunate truth is that my feelings are not touched or influenced by what I *really* am, by my actual beauty and goodness as God has made me. What touches my feelings, unfortunately, is *my perception* of what I'm really like. I am touched and influenced by how I see myself through the filters that I carry with me from my past life, those locked-in perceptions and prejudices which distort and disfigure my vision of myself. This is terribly important for me to understand. My feelings react not to the objective reality of what I am but to my *subjective* reality, to my perception of what I am.

Suppose, for example, that we view ourselves according to the Hollywood standard of beauty. Wow! That is disastrous for our self-esteem because by that standard most of us feel awfully plain and unattractive. We are not a Bo Derek or a Robert Redford. So we end up feeling terrible about ourselves. What have we done? We've used the wrong filter! The true measurement of a woman's beauty is not the features of her face or the measurement of her figure. A woman could have a perfect figure and yet act like a vicious and hateful person! And conversely, she could be overweight and very plain, yet be absolutely beautiful in her personality and in her responsiveness to others. The true measure of her beauty is the degree of her warmth, of her care and her sensitivity to the feelings of others, the measure of her heart. And the same is true for a man. The true measure of manliness is the measure of his courage and gentleness, *not* the measure of his height or his looks.

My perceptive system may be defined, therefore, as *my way* of *interpreting* the realities of my inner and outer worlds as I see them through my own special *series of filters*. My perceptive system offers me subjective reality, *my* reality; reality as it appears to me in counter-distinction to *objective* reality; to reality as it actually is.

My perceptive system, therefore, plays an absolutely fundamental role in my personality. Upon my perceptions depends the way in which I look upon myself and feel about myself. If my perceptions about the world and people are distorted, I have great difficulty relating well with people and thus achieving the needs of my world system. If my perceptions about myself are distorted, I am a prime subject for psychic pain. I am almost certain to despise myself.

Distorted Perceptions from Our Culture

It isn't only from our early life experiences that we have gathered a baggage of filters which distort our perceptions. We have formed many filters from the culture in which we are immersed.

It would be enlightening to trace the origins of such filters in detail. To understand, for example, the wholesale extent to which the mass media of movies, television, modern novels and newspapers have really seduced us into accepting the Hollywood superficial and distorted. How the business world has sold us its dictums that aggressiveness is the surest path to success and wealth, and that it is wealth which gives us prestige and happiness. How politicians have warped our notions about power and sold us on the necessity for expediency and deceit. How the Madison Avenue advertising establishment has all but convinced us that "new" is beautiful and "old" is ugly, that youth is attractive, middle age is stagnant and old age helpless and useless. One can just imagine the amount of psychic pain resulting from those perceptions!

To treat all of this adequately, however, would take us beyond the scope of this short study. For our purposes here, let us consider first the nature of our perceptive system, then the various kinds of filters which distort our perceptions and, finally, the tremendous impact of our perceptive system upon our inner and outer worlds.

The Nature of Perception

Perception, as I see it, is much more than an idea or an intellectual concept. Ideas are relatively easy to change. Most perceptions are very hard to change. If, for example, I think that two plus two equals five, it is fairly easy for you to convince me that two plus two is really four. If I have an inferiority complex, if I see myself incompetent and inadequate, it is extremely difficult for you to change that perception and convince me that the opposite is true. Even if you point out sizable accomplishments that I've achieved, I still say, "But I *feel* that I was just lucky in those cases! I feel inadequate."

Perception is more than an idea. Perception is an intellectual *vision* with roots more or less deeply implanted in my feelings. My perception of reality is *my way* of seeing that reality. It is my interpretation of reality.

Perception may be defined, therefore, as one's vision of reality, as that reality *appears* to be when it is seen through one's own special series of filters.

If I am wearing green-colored glasses, then everything around me looks green to me. Different shades of green, but green nevertheless. Things look green to me, not because they are green in themselves, in their true and objective reality. They may be yellow, blue, orange, purple. They look green to me simply because I am perceiving them through a green-colored filter. And if I were allergic to the color green, then I'd have an allergic reaction because as I see things now, they are green to me. My feelings react not to the objective reality but to my inner reality, to my perceptions of reality.

The truth is that I have a *whole series of filters* through which I look at the world around me, and through which I also look at myself. Some of those filters, as we saw above, come from the culture in which I am immersed. Most of them are the by-products of my past life, my past relationships, my past experiences, my past education, especially my whole experience of my parents.

Various Kinds of Filters

I have three different types of filters and, therefore, three different types of perceptions. The first are locked-in filters, those which are extremely hard to remove because they are deeply entrenched in my personality. Examples of such perceptions are my *attitudes*, my *ideals* (realistic and unrealistic), my *prejudices* and my *deep convictions*.

Perceptions coming from filters such as these are most difficult to change. They usually go back to very early experiences in my life or were formed by significant traumatic experiences that have left a deep mark (filter) in my consciousness. Many of these filters are the opinions, ideals, expectations, and prejudices which I experienced in my parents and in other significant persons. Through the years I have incorporated or introjected these persons into myself with all their locked-in filters intact. As a result those filters have now become almost a permanent part of me. Changing them and the feelings which follow from them is an extremely difficult task, even when I know intellectually that they are warped and distorted.

For example, Alice, a Sister in her early fifties, feels terribly ashamed about her prejudice toward black people. Intellectually she sees prejudice as unchristian and certainly unfair to an entire group of people. Alice would love to root out that prejudice from her personality. Nevertheless, every time she passes a black person on the street, an uneasy feeling of fear grips her. And, if the black person makes *any* gesture that looks threatening, Alice goes into a cold sweat of panic.

Her locked-in filter goes back to the time when she was a girl of twelve and a group of black girls threatened to beat her up. Actually, they did not hurt her physically, but the awful fright that she experienced at that time left an almost indelible filter in her personality, a filter which makes her perceive black people as a threat.

It is our locked-in filters, our semi-permanent perceptions which cause the greatest amount of psychic pain. They are also the most impervious to change. Sister Rose, for example, a woman in mid-life, would appear to anyone who knew her as a very capable and efficient executive. She started a human service organization in her parish which reaches out to the sick and homebound, to the poor and to the emotionally distraught. She is gracious to her volunteer workers, trains them for the work with a gentle firmness and imparts to them something of her own reverence for the suffering and the poor. Even though her main task now is administration, she makes time to be present at the right moment for those little acts of thoughtfulness that make the poor see her gifts to them as genuine care rather than a "handout."

Anyone outside herself would see Sister Rose as a brilliant organizer and a capable administrator. She does not, however, see herself that way, or at least she has not seen herself that way until recently. Her inferiority feelings go back to grammar school and to her experience with an impatient and harsh teacher who called her "stupid" and often insulted her in front of the class. Rose was a very sensitive child. The experience was traumatic for her. It left her with a distorted filter through which she saw herself as incapable of learning. And that perception, with all the ugly feelings about herself that followed from it, persisted right up until recent years, in spite of overwhelming evidence to the contrary in the form of brilliant personal achievements.

Mobile Filters

I have a second group of filters, *transference* and *counter-transference*, which might be more aptly described as mobile rather than as locked-in or semi-permanent. They are part of my "baggage," so to speak, but they do not distort my vision all the time. They do not fall into place before my mind unless and until they are projected there by a triggering mechanism.

Let me explain. Transference is a filter by which I experience you in my present life as though you were someone from my past life: father, mother, sibling. It is an unconscious filter. I have no idea that it is present. It is also dormant, off to the side, so to speak, and not coloring my intellectual vision. But once you occupy a position of authority over me, or act in some way similar to the way one of my parents acted, then that position or action triggers my transference filter and projects it into place before my mind. I now perceive you (unconsciously) as mother or father. And I react to you with many of the feelings that I had for that parent! I experience toward you many of the same expectations, same fears, same hopes that I experienced years ago toward my mother or father.

Sean, for example, a priest in his early forties, lived his childhood years with a great deal of fear. Both parents were very demanding of him, especially his mother. She never seemed pleased by what he did, in spite of strenuous efforts on his part to live up to her expectations. His marks should have been better, his room kept neater, his response to orders more prompt.

Sean experienced transference feelings for his superiors in religious life. He heard suggestions as commands and encouragements as demands to do better. As a consequence he re-lived in community much of the same painful feelings of resentment and frustration that he had experienced in childhood.

When I experience parental transference like this, I also have feelings about myself now that I used to have as a child in reference to my parents, whatever those feelings may have been. I may feel scolded by you, blamed by you, not listened to by you, as though you were actually doing those things to me. The filter of my transference makes me see your requests as demands, your interest in me as checking-up on me, your suggestion for my good as criticism and blame.

Sometimes the transference is *positive*, and then I expect you to love me and to care for me, to meet all my needs, to surround me with protection, and to anticipate all my wants and desires. This is how I remember my parents. *They* care for me this way. Since I now see you as parent, I have the same expectations of you! All those feelings are unrealistic now. They belong to my childhood and not to my present relationship with you. I do not know that they are unrealistic! And you have no idea why I'm making such outlandish demands of you!

Whether my transference filter is positive or negative, it makes me react with inappropriate and distorted feelings toward you. It makes me have expectations about you that are unreal. Obviously, such perceptions and feeling can cause a great deal of misunderstanding between you and me. You ask me a question and I hear it as an interrogation, a demand. You fail to understand something I've said, and I see it as a rejection. And my expectations of you are something you can never possibly fulfill.

Mary, a single woman in her mid-thirties, felt that her mother favored her brother who had studied for the priesthood. Mary felt that she had overlooked her and her needs. If Mary made a suggestion, her mother didn't go along with it. Mary felt that she didn't even hear it. If her brother, the priest, made the same suggestion, her mother responded with great warmth and enthusiasm. This hurt Mary a great deal. She often would say in her counseling sessions that she felt like an orphan.

When her transference toward me developed during the counseling relationship, it was a *maternal* transference. (It made no difference that I was a man! The sex of the person who triggers the transference is immaterial to the transference filter.) She constantly accused me of not listening to her, of not caring how she felt. The truth of the matter was that I felt very deeply for her pain. It hurt me that she had been so emotionally deprived. I listened very closely to what she said. But because of the negative transference, the slightest gesture on my part that seemed like a distraction would throw her into a rage. I had become "mother" and in me she re-experienced all the pain and "rejection" that she had experienced at home.

Even a positive transference can cause conflicts in a present relationship. Josephine, for example, a sister in her early thirties, obtained a position as parish minister in a parish with a pastor who was kind but emotionally distant. Josephine had loved her own father dearly but he died when she was only twelve. All her memories of him were positive, tender memories of care and affection and admiration. To her at twelve, her father was perfect. In her memories of him, at thirty-three, he was still perfect.

She developed, quite naturally, a paternal transference for the pastor and felt very warm and loving toward him. This, however, was a real problem for him. He was a man who was shy and emotionally distant toward everyone but especially toward women who were attractive. Josephine was a very attractive woman. So when she reached out in a warm and friendly way toward him, he became terrified. Apparently, he had no idea how to respond to her except to push her away emotionally. This hurt Josephine very much. She had absolutely no idea why he was so frightened because her own affection was truly innocent and honorable.

She was terribly disappointed in him. He "wasn't the kind of man she thought he was!" Even after she gained insight into the nature of her transference feelings and understood why she was so disappointed because he was not "father," her pain was so great that she had to leave the parish and get another assignment.

This whole case was sad because both she and the pastor were very fine people and very dedicated. If it had not been for the distorted perceptions caused by her transference filter and the inappropriate feelings which followed from it, they probably would have made a great parish team.

Fleeting Filters

The final group of filters that can mar and distort my perceptions are those fleeting and fairly easily removed filters which can arise through misunderstanding of words and misinterpretations of actions in my everyday dealings with other people. So, for example, suppose I ask you if you had a good time with your friend on your day off. I ask you to tell me all about it, where you went and what you did. My questions are motivated by interest and concern. I like you and I want you to know that I care.

Suppose, however, you hear my questions as motivated by curiosity or worse, that you see them as the "third degree" questioning of a district attorney. Wow! Instead of being pleased by my interest and concern, you are wild with anger over my brazen invasion of your privacy.

Your perception in this case is distorted by a filter. You interpret the objective reality of my concern as something entirely different, as insensitive curiosity and nerve. As long as that filter remains in place, it can cause painful feelings for us both. You are outraged about my "invasion" of your private world. And, for my part, I am deeply hurt that you are accusing me of intentions that I never had.

This type of filter is less serious than the others because it is easier to remove. As soon as I experience your annoyance at my question, I know in a moment that you are mis-reading me. So I can quickly clarify my question. "I'm sorry that you're offended. I don't mean to pry. I like you and I'm just sincerely interested in whether or not you had a good time." And, if you are reasonably open to me and can believe me, then the misunderstanding vanishes and the awful feelings with it.

Feelings Follow Perceptions

These, then, are the three types of filters that are almost continually projecting themselves before my intellectual "eyes," distorting in various ways and in varying degrees my perception of the truth. They distort the true vision of both my outer world and my inner world.

It is no wonder that Pilate exclaimed, "Truth! What is truth?" It's no wonder that epistemologists all through the centuries have struggled with the question, "Can we ever find the truth?" They were so aware that so much of what we see "out there" is *our own stuff*, distortions produced by our various filters. As we'll see later on, the work of recognizing our filters and removing as many of them as we can is really the journey toward truth and freedom, the journey Jesus Himself described when He said, "You shall know the truth, and the truth shall make you free!"

Meanwhile, it's very important for me to understand these three things. Firstly, that my perceptions depend directly and infallibly on my filters. Until I am able to recognize my filters and remove them, my mind perceives everything through them. I perceive, therefore, only part of the objective reality. The remaining part of my perception is the distortion produced by my filters.

Secondly, I must realize that my feelings follow infallibly upon my perceptions. If I perceive you as trying to poison me, I'm as terrified and as angry at you as if you really were trying to poison me. The objective fact that you have no intentions of hurting me doesn't really touch me or my feelings. My feelings are touched by

my perceptions with all their distortions. Feelings are not free to
follow my perceptions or not. Feelings are immediate, spontaneous
reactions to reality, as I perceive the reality.

Thirdly, it follows that the only way for me to change my
feelings is to change my perceptions.

The interaction of filters, perceptions and feelings might be
diagrammed this way:

Diagram 4.
My Perceptive System With the Distorting Filters

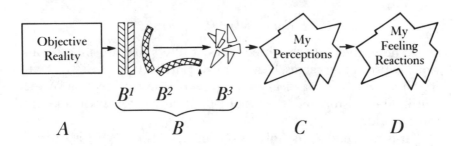

In this diagram, *A* represents the shape and texture of objective
reality, the real world of persons and things as they actually are. *B*
represents the three kinds of filters which distort our vision.

B^1 represents the locked-in filters;

B^2 —*our mobile filters of transference and countertransference (in the
diagram one has already been triggered into place; the second is still dormant);*

B^3—*our fleeting filters.*

C represents my perceptions of the real world showing how
distorted the real world looks to me because of my filters. Finally, *D*
represents my feeling reactions to the real world, showing how my
feelings are an *exact duplication* of my perceptions. Because my perceptions are distorted, so are my feelings.

Real growth and freedom come when I search out and remove
the various filters. Only then will my perceptions see people and
things as they really are and only then will my feelings be completely appropriate and on target.

Diagram 5.
My Perceptive System Without Distortions

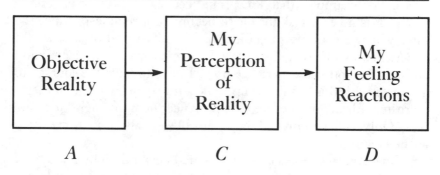

This diagram represents how I would be if I were completely filter-free. My perceptions—*C*—of the real world and other people would be *exactly* the *same* as the world and people are in themselves—*A*. I would see what is really there in my outer world without any exaggeration or distortion. My feelings, therefore—*D*—would also be proportionate to reality. They would neither be too much nor too little, not inappropriate in any way. I would see what's really there and my feelings would react to that reality and to nothing else. I would be *free* at last!

Of course, in all probability no one ever reaches this degree of freedom in this life. It will only be in heaven, when we see God in the beatific vision and behold all else in His clear and beautiful light, that we will be completely filter-free. Until then some built-in filters will probably remain in us, as well as the continual possibility of transference and counter-transference. Achieving freedom in this life is a journey in which we remove as many distortions as we can!

No Easy Task

This is no easy job—this pursuit of self-knowledge, this clearing out of filters. Many times we are not even conscious of the fact that our perceptions are distorted. Something looks unfair to me, so most times I simply pre-suppose that this is how it really is—unfair!

I have no idea that I have obscured the reality because of my filters. Even when I am conscious that I'm distorting the truth, when I am aware, for example, that I'm prejudiced against a certain ethnic group, it is no easy task for me to become unprejudiced. Since the filter which causes my prejudice was manufactured by a powerful experience in my past life, I need to open myself to a new and corrective emotional experience now. I have to have the courage to associate with this ethnic group, talk with them, work with them, recreate with them, in order to experience them in a new, accurate way. Only then will my old filter crumble and allow me to see them as they really are.

Mike, a priest in his late thirties, had been raised by immigrant Irish parents who were suspicious and afraid of people with Spanish background. They used disparaging language in describing Latin Americans, such as "spics," "greasy," "knife-throwers." As a result, Mike grew up with a locked-in filter which made him almost equally as prejudiced.

About six years after ordination he was sent to Puerto Rico to study Spanish and then assigned to an inner-city parish which was mostly Spanish-speaking. He was terrified at first and defensive. His own rigid control of his feelings only helped to make him more suspicious of these people who expressed their feelings so freely.

Gradually, the warmth of the Spanish people began to touch him. They appreciated his sincerity and they showed him that they did with evident affection. In less than a year's time he had an entirely new experience of Spanish people and Spanish culture. He not only changed his prejudices; he also changed his own stiffness and rigid control of his feelings.

When the locked-in perceptions are about *myself*, when I have an inferiority complex, for example, or a feeling of powerlessness, then the task of rooting out the negative filters is more difficult still. Here also my filter was created by an experience in childhood, at an age when I was very impressionable. So, here too, I need a powerful, corrective emotional experience to change my false impressions (filters) of inferiority and powerlessness. Since it is now my self-esteem, however, which is hurt so badly, I am extremely fearful of taking the risk to be open to a new emotional experience of my ability or my power. I'm too suspicious that my early experience will only be verified and make me feel even worse!

The procedures I can take to help me on this journey to self-knowledge will be outlined in greater detail in Chapter VII: "Rebuilding Self-Esteem." Meantime it will help me to prepare for that searching out process if I study some examples of my most common filters.

Perceptions About My Outer World
False Attitudes

Many of my perceptions about other people are colored by my locked-in filters. Unfortunately, there are so many of these attitudes and prejudices that it's not possible to describe them all in the limited scope of this study. It is certainly worth my while, however, to look at some of them, especially those which seem to occur fairly often.

One young priest, Fred, looked upon other people with an attitude that could only be described as a "chip-on-the- shoulder." When he came to group for the first time, he pulled his chair back toward the wall, folded his arms in a defensive and drawn-back stance and announced, "I'm just here in the group to check it out. If I don't like it, I'm not going to stay!" The atmosphere in the group was immediately charged with tension.

When the others expressed their dismay at his attitude of apparent belligerence, he told how he had been in combat in Vietnam before studying for the priesthood. He recounted one "dirty-deal" after another that he had suffered at the hands of junior officers; told how he had become so completely disillusioned about his officers that he even found himself giving his approval when men in his squad planned to kill their sergeant. He told how he learned from bitter experience that each person has to look out for himself. Everyone was guilty in his eyes until proven innocent! Actually, his chip-on-the-shoulder began many years before Vietnam, began in some of the painful experiences of his early life.

The members of the group were very wary of him for at least a couple of months. He wouldn't speak in terms of simply feeling anger. He'd speak in terms of acting-out his anger, of "running people through with a hunting knife!" A good deal of this exaggeration, of course, was a mask but it reflected his basic attitudes that "no one is to be trusted" and that "no one is going to push him around."

The sad part of his attitude is that the members of the group were gentle and sensitive people who didn't want to push anyone around. And eventually their gentleness and concern touched him and his whole manner toward them changed into one of care and respect. He was fortunate to have met such a fine group of people. In another setting the group members could easily have reacted negatively to his belligerent attitude and fought back. And, of course, this would only have served to convince him that he was right all the time, that people can't really be trusted.

Another common attitude, one that is similar to the chip-on-the-shoulder, is the perception that "No one really gives a damn for anyone else. Everybody is just out for himself!" Jane, a middle-aged high school teacher, was a clear example of a person with this attitude. That's how she saw people. The only exceptions, oddly enough, were her students. She was able to enter into their world beautifully, and, therefore, was a very capable teacher.

Everyone over the high school age was a selfish hateful person in her eyes. She used to have a different attitude, she admitted. She had "gone out of her way countless times to do favors for others." (This was true. She had been very generous! But *God help anyone* who didn't respond immediately with equal generosity!) Now, however, she was "wiser." She had been hurt too many times ever to be convinced again that some people could care.

The *fierceness* of the *anger* she felt as a result of this attitude is hard to describe. And yet she could *not* admit that she was angry. So the energy of her anger came out "sideways" in many snide remarks, inappropriate sighs, and in facial expressions that made her look as though she could kill.

When others would talk about their painful feelings in the group, she didn't hear their pain or feel empathy for them. Instead she would roll her eyes up to the ceiling and very audibly give a sigh which clearly said: "Oh, come on! Get off it!" At other times she'd unwrap noisy candy wrappers while others told a story so painful that they were dissolved in tears. Some of the people in the group reacted to that with anger. "Why do you come if you are so bored?" She said, "Because Jim made me come!" I could hardly believe her words. I said: "I have that power?" Obviously I didn't. She was coming because deep down she was hoping against hope that we would understand her and care for her. And yet her attitude made it next to impossible for her to believe that we *did* care.

We certainly tried, each one of us, but we got nowhere! Each time we reached out to touch her pain with understanding and concern, she would *deny* pain.

Once, for example, when I responded to the pain of another woman in the group, Jane said, "Oh look! There goes Daddy defending his little girl!" It was a fresh remark and very insensitive to the pain of the other woman. And yet I realized how hurt Jane must have been herself. So I said, "Jane, if you feel that I care for others more than I do for you, I can understand how much that must hurt you!" No good! Complete denial! "That doesn't bother me!" she answered with a shrug that said, "Don't flatter yourself to think that you are that important to me!"

We made no discernible progress with Jane. Eventually she left the group apparently convinced that we were the same as everyone else. "Nobody really gives a damn! All are out for themselves!" This locked-in attitude distorted frightfully her perception of other people, and her *feelings* reacted to her perception rather than to the way the people in the group really were.

A third and a very frequent attitude is the filter that might aptly be described as "all-or-nothing," the filter which blocks out from my vision all the middle ground between the extremes. So, for example, if you don't agree with everything I hold dear, then I see you as entirely against my opinions and my values. You are not entirely against me, of course! There are many values that we have in common. But when I see you through my "all-or-nothing" filter, I don't even notice what we have in common. You are against my plan for renewal in the parish, so you are against *me*! So, how can I possibly put up with you! We obviously cannot work together. We are at opposite ends of the pole!

This is so sad. When I perceive you in this way, I not only deprive you of a fair hearing, but I also deprive myself of all the support you could give me in the areas where we think alike. I also lose out on all the insights and new points of view that I could get from you in the areas where we think differently.

All too often I approach my interpersonal relationships with this same destructive filter. Either you are a friend one hundred percent of the way or forget it! You are no friend at all! You have to understand me completely, respond to my every need, be always available to my beck and call, or else, how can you say that you are my friend! I never even notice all the time you *are* there for me, all the understanding and care that you do give. I just notice that sometimes you don't understand. So that's it! "Sometimes" becomes "always," because I only see "all-or-nothing."

And when the "all-or-nothing" filter is used to view my inner world, then the damage in terms of psychic pain is devastating! No person, with the exception of Jesus, could possibly measure up to that yardstick of "all-or-nothing." We will look at this more fully when we discuss some of the faulty perceptions in our inner world.

Prejudices in My Outer World

Sometimes my filters make me prejudiced against certain races and ethnic groups, against people with a different life-style or different political convictions, even against those of the opposite sex! It's like putting a whole group of people in a pigeon hole from which I allow them no escape.

"Don't ever trust the Jews," I hear myself saying. "They are an aggressive and deceitful people. And watch out for the Arabs as well. They'd steal the fillings from your teeth! Germans are all thick and stubborn. The Irish are all drunkards. The Italians and French are all womanizers.

"The cops are out to get you, not to protect you. Don't trust them! Doctors are all out for money. They do not really care about people. Hippies are all immature and dirty. Lawyers are all crooked. There can never be any litigation in heaven because all the lawyers are in hell.

"The British are all snobs. The Poles are all dumb. Americans have dollar signs for eyes. Bankers have no hearts. Salesmen never tell the truth; politicians don't even know the truth from a lie!"

All of these filters distort my perceptions to a degree that is harrowing. All the members of these groups become the guiltless victims of my snide remarks and cold actions. They have been *prejudged* by me, seen in a pejorative light, entirely apart from the objective truth of who they are and what they are like. And since my actions follow my feelings, I often treat them terribly as well.

Sometimes my prejudice runs against the members of the opposite sex. Too often men see women as basically evil and deceitful. Because they have felt themselves betrayed by one woman, they conclude that all women are the same—cruel, deceitful, hypocritical. This kind of man turns off all women. It does not matter to him that this present woman who likes him is genuine and sincere. He does not even see the objective reality of how she really is; he only sees his own filter—the pain and bitterness of his past experiences.

Unfortunately, many women return the "compliment" and look down on men. They see men as power-hungry and insensitive to women. Sometimes they see men as "animals" who only desire a woman for sex and nothing else. The bitter feelings that flow from such a prejudiced perception are felt for *all* men, no matter how gentle, loving and sensitive this particular man in her life may be. All men get smeared with the same dark paint of selfishness and insensitivity.

Such a woman finds it near to impossible to form a warm love relationship with a man. It does not matter how much he may really like her and admire her. Her prejudice sees his honest offer of friendship as just another seduction to use her and abuse her.

Regretfully, such prejudices can even affect my perception of my own sex. If a young boy constantly hears his mother ridiculing and putting-down his father, if he hears her warn his sisters not to trust men because "men are only out for one thing," then quite possibly he will grow up with the same prejudice about men as his mother had. He will find it hard to make men-friends, hard to reveal himself to another man or trust another man. He finds himself only relaxed and self-disclosing when he is relating to a woman. Half of the population of his world has been effectively cut off from him.

Too many women also experience this kind of prejudice against their own sex. They pre-judge women as catty and jealous and deceitful. They cannot believe that a woman can truly be a loyal friend to another woman. Consequently, they cannot be happy except in the company of men and thus they are deprived of a whole world of emotional support and care from members of their own sex.

Locked-in filters are sometimes conscious, oftentimes unconscious, but almost always they are damaging. They warp our perceptions and cause inappropriate feelings. They lead us to speak to others without reverence and to treat others in ways that wound them and alienate them.

Mobile Filters

It isn't only the locked-in filters of my attitudes and prejudices that hinder me from fulfilling the needs of my outer world. I also carry within me the "baggage" of *mobile filters*—filters which at a moment's notice can fall into place before my vision and further distort my perception of reality. These filters, as we saw above, are transference and counter-transference.

Such filters form in me a series of *unrealistic expectations*, *unwarranted fears* and *unreasonable hostility* on the one hand and, on the other hand, *unrealistic love feelings* and *unreasonable demands*. All these are the by-products of my childhood experiences with my mother, father and siblings. They are *mobile* rather than locked into place, in the sense that *ordinarily* they do *not* come between my vision and the external reality. Ordinarily they are off to the side, so to speak, until a triggering mechanism releases the lock that holds them out of the way and they then spring into place.

So, ordinarily I do not perceive you through the filter of my mother or father. And therefore I do *not* expect you to treat me the way they did. I do not fear you in the way I feared *them* as a child. I am not angry at you for the frustrations and punishments that my parents caused me. I do not expect you to fulfill all my needs.

All you have to do, however, is assume a position of authority over me, or even an *air* of authority, talk like them, smile like them, act like them, and pow! You trigger the catch that holds my transference filter off to the side and immediately it springs into place between *you* and my *vision* of you. It happens without any conscious awareness on my part. I have no idea *why* I now see you differently, hear you differently, and have a whole new set of *feelings* about you. In my perceptions and feelings, I am now back in childhood, and I actually expect from you the same attitudes, corrections, orders, put-downs, support, affirmation, etc. that I received from my mother or my father, depending on which filter was triggered. The resulting distortions in my perceptions, my feelings and my actions can frightfully short-circuit the interaction between us and woe-fully confuse our relationship.

Susan, a fine young Sister, was a striking example of the distor-tions that transference can cause. She was a social worker and therefore well acquainted with the phenomenon of transference in others, but she was completely unaware of her paternal transfer-ence feelings toward me in our counseling relationship. Her dad had been an excellent provider for his family and a warm support for his children in all their problems. He seemed to know just what to say and what to do for every ache and pain.

When Susan came for counseling in order to deal with her relational problems in community life, her expectations of me were very similar to the expectations she had of her father when she was a little girl. Unfortunately, I did not have her father's "magic." Even if I did, I knew that the woman in Susan would not want *me* to solve her problems. She would want to solve her own problems. I also knew that the answers to her problems were really inside her. My job was to help her to find them.

Once the transference grew strong, however, she became furi-ous at me because I "knew the correct words to solve the problem and I was deliberately holding back from saying them!" It was remarkable! The professional woman in her knew differently—but the little girl in her "needed" her father to say the magic words and make her problem go away.

That moment was the appropriate time for the interpretation of her transference and the beginning of the process of her working through the false perceptions and childish dependency which she had for all authority figures. But, if the situation had been other than that of counseling, perhaps neither she nor the authority figure would have understood what was happening. Susan would have simply been frustrated and hurt. And the authority figure might have given up on her as a "dependent little girl."

Counselors and therapists are not immune from transference filters and feelings. In their case it is called counter-transference because often the triggering mechanism for their filter is the trans-ference reactions of their clients. Such counter-transference reac-tions happen quite often also to priests in their parishes and to religious in their schools. Their very role as "Father," "Sister," "Brother" makes them authority figures and sets them up for transference feelings from their parishioners and students. It is awfully important that priests and religious understand this so that they don't get *trapped* into counter-transference behavior. They need to see the unwarranted hostility toward them for what it really is, the rage hanging over from a parishioner's childhood and now projected onto them. They need to understand that the romantic "crush" of a parishioner or student is an unconscious need for a good father or a good mother.

Such transference projections from parishioners and students can not only be painful in themselves for the religious person, but can also trigger counter-transference reactions in him. Once that happens the priest no longer sees his parishioner as the hurting person that she is, a person suffering from unconscious hostility. Instead the priest makes the parishioner someone from *his own past life* from whom he has suffered unwarranted anger. And the priest himself now *over-reacts*. He gets furious at her. She is an "ingrate" who doesn't appreciate all that he has tried to do for her. She also has "some damn nerve" being angry at him when he has been so kind to her. So she can just go and fry ice!

Distorted perceptions and feelings are now working full blast in both persons. The results can be unbelievable confusion and pain, where both priest and parishioner are reacting with violent feelings that belong to *someone else* from their past rather than reacting to each other. And both suffer hurts that are unrealistic and unnecessary.

Once the priest and religious have an understanding of the nature of transference reactions in their parishioners and students, they are able to avoid counter-hostility to the parishioner's anger and avoid a paternalistic reaction in response to the student's "crush."

Perceptions About My Inner World
Unrealistic Ego-Ideal

If locked in filters can cause havoc in my outer world relationships, they can be the source of *incredible psychic pain* in my inner world feelings about myself.

Probably the most frequent locked-in filters center around my *ego-ideal*, the attitudes I have absorbed over the years about the *kind of person* that I *imagine I ought to be*. If that ideal is unrealistically high, then I have an *inbuilt well of psychic pain*, a well of guilt and inadequate feelings by which I excoriate myself for not being this super-human person.

One of these filters is the false ideal of *perfectionism*. "If a thing is worth doing, it is worth doing *perfectly."* When this *ideal* "teams up" with my "all-or-nothing" attitude, as it often does, then I am in deep trouble. *Who*, except Jesus, could *possibly* do anything *perfectly* in this life? *No one can*! But my filter doesn't realize that. My perfectionistic filter *expects* me to be *perfect*. And when I *fail* to be perfect, I view myself as *nothing* but a *failure*. Not even *part* failure! I'm a *complete failure*. What an insufferable person!

I may be a brilliant teacher, plan my classes thoroughly, present them with vitality and clarity, make myself available to my students for any questions or for any private help. *But* in spite of all that I do, some get poor marks on the test and some fail. This is the normal curve of success and failure which is to be expected in any class!

When I'm the victim of a perfectionistic filter, however, how do I see this normal curve in my class? I see it as an ugly reflection on my ability as a teacher. I not only feel like a poor teacher; I now feel that I am a *disaster*! I don't give myself any credit for the students who have passed with brilliant marks. I don't even advert to the fact that it is these students who are the more accurate measure of my teaching ability! I can't see that! "If a thing is worth doing, it's worth doing perfectly!" My classes could not have been perfect, so obviously I'm a failure!

It is even more painful for me when this ideal evaluates my moral conduct. Then guilt feelings just torture me! I may have fought temptation ten times and succeeded. But I don't even see my successes. They don't count. All I can see is my failure. I'm not just slightly bad because I failed this one time. I'm all bad! I'm no good! I lose self-esteem because I failed to reach "the unreachable star" of absolute perfection—an ego ideal that is unattainable even for good people in this nature of ours that has been wounded by original sin.

God doesn't have those filters. He has said so in many ways that He is pleased with my struggle. He understands my failures. He forgives me with infinite compassion and says: "My son, you were lost but now you are found!" But I can't even see Him or His compassion. My distorted perception only lets me see my miserable failures," and I wallow in the murky waters of self-pity and self-blame, tortured by psychic pain!

It would be more Christian and more healthy to feel: "If a thing is worth doing, it is worth doing poorly!" Better to do it in my own human and limited way than not to do it at all.

Another filter which often distorts my perception of myself is the attitude that any sort of needing on my part makes me a child rather than an adult, a perception which causes an immediate feeling reaction of inadequacy and powerlessness.

Agnes, a novice in her mid-twenties, developed a fairly serious cold. She felt miserable. But, when her novice mistress, in a gesture of genuine concern, offered her Vicks and some aspirin, Agnes brushed both of them aside with evident annoyance, "It's no big deal! I'm all right!" Needing help, in her perception, made one a dependent child, so she couldn't accept the kindness and thoughtfulness of her Mistress. The act of love from the Mistress could not be completed because instead of seeing it as an act of love for her as an adult, Agnes perceived it as an act of pity for a child.

There is a kind of dependency, of course, which is childish, the dependency which says in effect, "Feed me, take care of me, solve my every problem, because I can't do anything for myself!" This helpless dependency is appropriate in childhood but is neither appropriate nor psychologically healthy in adults.

There is another kind of dependency, however, which is not only healthy in adults but also absolutely necessary before an adult is able to love. This is adult dependency and it says to its loved ones, "You mean a great deal to me. My life would be terribly empty without your care and affection. I really need you!" *This* kind of dependency is a beautiful gift to our loved ones. Far from being childish, it is eminently mature.

Our perception gets distorted when we have the locked-in filter which sees all dependency as childish dependency. Once we make that mistake, then our defenses cannot bear to be dependent even in an adult fashion. And we put on airs of a rugged independence, as though we don't need anybody or anything! And as the song put it so neatly, "We become more like children than children!" The truth is that "people who need people are the luckiest people in the world."

All too many priests and religious fail to achieve warm interpersonal relationships because of this distorted attitude. They confuse mature dependency with childish dependency. So, in their struggle to grow mature, they throw out both of them. They can never need others. They cannot accept favors, cannot ask for help, cannot reach out for affection. The only feelings which they admit are positive feelings. Everything is always: "Oh, I'm fine, thanks!" "No thanks, I can manage: thank you for offering to help!" It's sad! They cannot let love touch them because "Needing is only for children!"

False attitudes about physical beauty cause immense psychic pain for many persons. And even here priests and religious are not exempt. The filters are many: Men must be tall and have a full head of hair; they must be muscular and yet slim, good looking in their facial features but not so good looking that they appear "pretty." Women must have an ample bust and full hips but be slim in the waist. They must have pretty facial features, flowing hair with evident bounce. They must not be too tall nor too short. And they must know how to dress in chic fashion and how to wear make-up.

These filters are a free "gift" from our culture. Unfortunately they set up a standard in my perceptive system by which I put my body on trial, judge it and often condemn it and myself along with it. If my body fails to meet any of these standards, I can easily perceive myself as unattractive, plain, homely—even distasteful and ugly. My real beauty and worth doesn't touch my feelings. I respond only to my distorted filters!

These cultural standards of beauty are especially powerful when the filters have been reinforced by significant persons in our early childhood.

Paul, for example, was short in stature even though his brothers and sisters were fairly tall. It bothered him that he was the shortest in the family and shorter than his high school friends. The fact that he was a good athlete and a good leader, however, somewhat compensated for his disappointment about his height. He threw himself energetically into sports, high school activities, parties and dances. He was a forceful speaker on the school debating team and won the silver medal at the oratorical contest. Generally speaking he felt popular with his peers.

One day, however, he expressed his anger to one of his brothers. His mother overheard the argument and said to him with a tone of disdain: "You're just the right size for a pup!" Paul staggered under this rebuke. He did not say another word. The pain that he felt was excruciating! He dearly loved his mother, but with one short sentence she had put-down both his feelings of anger and his body.

The change in his personality after that was severe and abrupt. He completely suppressed all expression of feeling, especially his angry feelings. He wouldn't even give expression to any opinions or preferences. According to this new filter, all assertion was bad, made him a "pup," so there would be no assertiveness on his part from then on! His teachers at school would ask, "Paul, what's happened to you!" The English professor, who listened to Paul's speech for the graduation ceremonies, complained: "Paul, this isn't you! You're lifeless! Come on, put some feeling into it!"

He had done something to "correct" his unacceptable anger. There was absolutely nothing, however, that he could do about his height! That poor body image and the loss of self-esteem that went with it lasted until his years of therapy much later in life. Therapy brought a new standard and with it a new self-acceptance.

These false standards of beauty are very detrimental to psychological health and happiness. My body image rightly or wrongly, is a powerful segment of my self-image. So, when I don't feel handsome or beautiful by these false standards, my image of myself suffers a serious blow. It's just very tragic that people can be absolutely beautiful persons by every true and valid standard, and yet feel plain or downright ugly because of a distorted set of filters!

Finally, there is one unrealistic ideal that causes me an immense amount of psychic pain—and that is the perception that certain feelings automatically make me bad—just by themselves, just by the fact that I feel them. Such feelings are anger, fear, jealousy, sexual arousal, frustration. It doesn't make any difference to my perception that I did not start these feelings! They are reactions, not actions! I am not responsible for them. I did not choose them. I do not want them. But this makes no difference to my false perception, the perception that concludes that I am ugly and bad just because I feel these "bad" feelings!

This is a completely unrealistic ideal. God made me to have such feelings as these not only as a defense against hostile forces, but also to add color and zest to my life as well as motivation. My feelings, all my feelings, are such an important part of me that I can truly say: "I am what I feel!" even more than I can say: "I am what I think!" or "I am what I do!" In my feelings are my likes and dislikes, my joys, my hopes, my fears, my ideals and aspirations, my loves.

Feelings in themselves cannot fairly be called "bad" or "good," because most often I do not start my feelings. My feelings are *reactions* to stimuli and follow from my perceptions. What *is* bad or good is how I handle my feelings. If I let them lead me to destructive behavior, then I deserve to feel guilty because that destructive behavior is morally bad.

So, for example, if I let my jealousy for you lead me to say libelous things about you and thus destroy your reputation; or, if I allow my anger to express itself in sarcasm and put-downs that make you feel stupid and inferior, then I have been morally wrong! Then I should feel guilty.

If instead of this "acting-out" my feelings, however, I own them, and I express them in a healthy, wholesome way; if I channel them into behavior that is loving and constructive, then my conduct is good. In a word, my actions can be bad or good; my feelings are not!

Feelings can only be either appropriate or inappropriate, i.e., they are either an accurate reaction to the objective reality, accurate in kind and degree, or an inaccurate reaction in kind or in degree. Suppose, for example, that you want to compliment me for having the courage of my convictions and you say, "Jim, you really stood your ground!" That's a nice compliment. I have an appropriate reaction to your words if I feel honored and pleased.

If I misinterpret your words, however, if I think you mean: "Jim, you're being as stubborn as a mule!" then I'd feel terribly hurt and angry. This reaction is inappropriate because it does not reflect what you really said. Note: My feeling hurt is not bad or good. I don't intentionally feel this way. But my feeling is inappropriate in kind.

Feelings can also be inappropriate in degree, either not strong enough or, as happens most often, too strong. If you give me fifty cents worth of aggravation, for example, and I react with five dollars worth of anger, then four dollars and fifty cents worth of my anger is exaggerated.

Well, this is the situation with my unrealistic ego-ideals. They cause me to look down on myself when I feel angry and jealous, as though just having those feelings makes me an ugly person. This reaction is inappropriate, both in kind and in degree. I'm blaming myself just for being a human being!

Notice that I'm really talking about two sets of feelings. The first I might call my *outer* feelings (even though I feel them inside myself) because they are reactions to my outer world of people and things. The second set of feelings I can call my *inner* feelings because they are reactions to my inner world, to my first set of feelings.

In other words, I not only have feelings about your hurting me and therefore get angry at you (an *outer* feeling) but almost immediately I have a *second* feeling, a feeling about the fact that I feel angry. Most often this second feeling is a feeling of guilt or shame, because most of us in our childhood have been trained to see anger as something bad. The first feeling is about you in my outer world. The second feeling is a feeling of psychic pain, because it is a feeling about *me*. I get angry with myself for feeling angry at you!

The diagram (#6) below demonstrates the interaction between these two sets of feelings. The first set are reactions to stimuli from my *outer* world; the second, to stimuli from my *inner world*.

Notice that my first set of feelings are the result of stimuli from outside myself, stimuli such as hurt, danger, the beauty and talents of another person. These stimuli cause me to react with the feelings of anger, fear, jealousy. These are perfectly normal reactions.

But, then, these very reactions become a *new set of stimuli*. I not only have these feelings about the outer world; I also have feelings about these feelings. And when these first feelings are perceived as ugly and bad through the filters of my unrealistic ideals, then the second set of feelings are extremely *negative and degrading*.

It is this set of *inner* world feelings that are the most painful because these feelings are about *me*. They wreak havoc with my self-esteem. I feel that I am guilty and ugly and helpless and stupid! And the tragic part about them is that they are inappropriate! I am not ugly or bad because I feel jealousy or sexual arousal! I am not cowardly because I react with fear to danger! God made me to react that way. Those first feelings help me to cope with the dangers in my life. These first feelings are realistic. It is only the second set of feelings that are inappropriate!

Diagram 6.

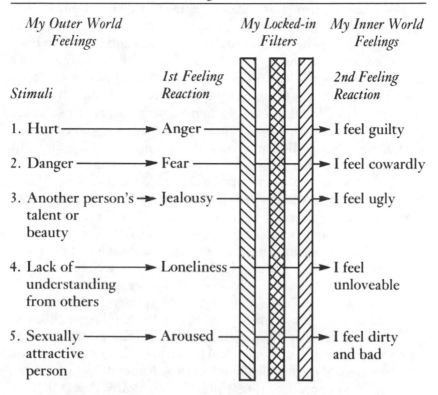

My Outer World Feelings		My Locked-in Filters	My Inner World Feelings
	1st Feeling Reaction		*2nd Feeling Reaction*
Stimuli			
1. Hurt	Anger		I feel guilty
2. Danger	Fear		I feel cowardly
3. Another person's talent or beauty	Jealousy		I feel ugly
4. Lack of understanding from others	Loneliness		I feel unloveable
5. Sexually attractive person	Aroused		I feel dirty and bad

I am really ugly or bad *only* if I let these feelings lead me to destructive behavior, if I allow my jealousy to lead me to refuse to be open to you or to abuse you physically. But it is this behavior that is bad, not my feelings.

I have experienced this kind of psychic pain very frequently in married couples as well as in priests and religious. Bob and Sandra, for example, came in for counseling because they were experiencing extreme pain in their relationship. Bob was a huge man physically but extremely controlled in his feelings, especially feelings that were soft and gentle. He lacked verbal fluency in expressing himself. He never seemed to say kind things to Sandra or the children. When he did speak, apparently it was only in the form of complaints and put-downs.

Sandra loved him, so his constant put-downs were extremely

painful to her. Unfortunately, she retaliated with derogatory remarks about his family and about his manhood. Even though her
verbal ability was much greater than his, she didn't use words to
express her hurt; she used words to attack him and disparage him.

Both were hurting terribly. Yet neither of them told the other
how hurt each was. Bob especially was ashamed of his hurt feelings. He felt that it was unmanly that her remarks could hurt him
so deeply. How could he express them to her when he felt so guilty
about them! And even though our culture allows women to feel
hurt more readily than it allows this to men, Sandra also felt
ashamed of her feelings, especially jealousy for his family.

I tried to help by expressing the hurt for them. I said: "Wow,
Bob, I'd feel terribly hurt if Sandra were my wife and she said those
things to me. I don't know if I could take it!" The expression on his
face was one of unbelievable relief. He had received "permission" to
be hurt! It was not unmanly. It *was* understandable! "Yes, I was
hurt," he said, "very hurt." He spoke with real feeling and tears
welled up in his eyes. This touched Sandra deeply. "I never knew
you cared that much," she said to him. "I never knew you cared," and
she cried openly. It was the beginning of a beautiful reconciliation.

They had hidden from each other their deepest feelings, feelings that could cure and mend their relationship, simply because
they perceived those feelings as something shameful!

I need to appreciate this! I need to see clearly that it is these
inner feelings of shame and guilt that are the inappropriate ones!
Then I will no longer feel this false shame and guilt. Shame will no
longer inhibit me. I'll be able to deal with my outer feelings in a
more healthy and constructive way. I'll be able to own them, express them in a gentle but assertive way with appropriate effect and
eventually I'll be able to let them go.

Unrealistic Role Ideals

Some of our more common locked-in filters pertain to our role
in life as priest or religious. Most often these filters were formed
through a spiritual training that was not completely sound psychologically. Well-meaning spiritual directors in seminaries and novi-
tiates encouraged their novices to ideals that were perfectionistic.
The directors were sincere and highly motivated. They didn't real-

ize for a moment that they were creating a built-in guilt system that would leave in its wake a huge trail of psychic pain.

Perhaps just a brief treatment of some of these "ideals" is all that we need to bring them to our awareness. The work ideal was a very common one. In one way or another we were told that we would "have to account for every idle moment." What a damper that could put on any attempt at leisure time! Leisure became something unnecessary and wasteful. One could not "waste time" in leisurely pursuits without feeling a bit guilty. Only if the leisure time were spent in cultural pursuits, reading good literature, listening to classical music, sewing or knitting, only then could we "justify" it as worthwhile.

The generosity "ideal" was another. Starting with St. Paul's admonition to be "all things to all men," many of us moulded that beautiful ideal of openness to all people into a rigid pharisaical burden. We imagined that we had to be present and attentive to everyone all the time. Ready at everyone's beck and call with total disregard for our own needs, our own privacy, our own solitude. An impossible ideal! Not even a devoted mother can be one hundred percent present to her child. And yet, when of necessity we took some time for ourselves, we felt selfish and guilty, felt that we were a far cry from the "ideal" apostle!

Years ago, Tony, a young priest from an inner city parish, came for counseling because he was very close to burn-out. In a rash gesture of false generosity, he and his associate priests had thrown open the rectory at all times, day and night, to their parishioners. They wanted the parishioners to know that the priests were there to serve them and to share their poverty. Not even their dining room or their bedrooms were off limits!

As a result there were very few hours day or night when there were not people walking through the rectory, getting themselves something to eat from the kitchen, walking into offices and bedrooms to talk about problems.

I let Tony express his utter exhaustion, and his "guilt" that he was beginning to resent people. Gradually I was able to question this "ideal." "Tony, even the poorest of the poor have some privacy in their own home, and time for meals and for sleep." Little by little his neurotic guilt feelings subsided and he was able to give himself permission to fulfill his own basic need.

All too many of us bought the "ideal" that celibates should be "sexless." We would acknowledge in words that celibates are human, and therefore are subject to sexual fantasies and feelings. We might even admit, if we were pressed to the wall, that occasionally even celibates might need a release from the build-up of sexual tension in the form of masturbation. But, when any of those fantasies or feelings came over us, all that intellectual acknowledgement did very little to lessen the psychic pain or our uneasiness and guilt. The unconscious filter was still locked-in, and it said that celibates must be something of a neuter gender.

Many even felt that celibates should also be friendless. They must be loving, but only in a very generalized fashion. No one must be special in the feelings of a true celibate. Particular friendships would only wean his or her affections away from God. This filter is less active today because of all the splendid material that has been written about the psychological and spiritual benefits of deep, interpersonal relationships. But for many years before Vatican II, a large percentage of religious would never allow themselves to have a close friend of either sex.

Depending on the nature of our years of formation and upon the relative psychological health of our spiritual directors, there are a number of other unrealistic role-ideals that are fairly common: Priests should never drink. Both priests and religious should be comfortable in experiencing squalor, or else there is something lacking in their spirit of poverty. Priests and religious should always be non-assertive, passive, submissive. If they speak up, especially if they speak up for their own rights, they are definitely lacking in humility and meekness.

Perhaps one of the most debilitating of all the unrealistic role-ideals is the "ideal" that neither priests nor religious should have close friends of the opposite sex, in spite of all the wonderful benefits that can flow from such a relationship. Celibate relationships are not really possible, according to this filter, and those who attempt to enter such relationships are only fooling themselves and causing great scandal besides!

There *are* dangers, of course, in any celibate relationship and it would be foolhardy not to own those dangers. There is real danger of genital involvement, danger of exclusiveness. There is a danger of possible loss of vocation as well as danger of scandal.

Celibates who honestly admit that these dangers are real, and work to make them remote, effectively change the risk involved from being a foolhardy risk. They avoid exclusiveness; they discuss their relationship honestly with a counselor or friend and they are careful not to flaunt their feelings for each other in the presence of others.

Once they take such precautions, their relationship brings about some absolutely lovely results in each of them. The first and foremost effect is a definite growth in their self-esteem. The joy of knowing that someone really loves them makes them feel beautiful and good. Often, also, their prayer life is endowed with a new warmth and clarity, a whole new sense of gratitude and appreciation of God's goodness and beauty. Usually there is a decided increase in joy, a joy which suffuses all that they do and simply radiates to all around them the Good News of Jesus. And finally, very often, both of them experience a whole new sense of relaxation and ease with members of the opposite sex in general, an ease which helps them considerably in their apostolate.

The possibility, more, the probability of such creative and beautiful results makes a celibate relationship something very worthwhile and desirable. It *is* a risk but it need not be a foolhardy risk. Once the celibate partners make the dangers remote by prudent and vigilant care, then the positive benefits that flow from a celibate relationship make it a *calculated risk*, a risk in which the proximate benefits far outweigh the remote dangers, a risk, therefore, which is eminently worth taking.

All of these unrealistic role ideals are pregnant with psychic pain. They form the "shoulds" and the "should nots" in our perceptive system, which makes us feel terribly about ourselves whenever we fail to live up to them.

Healthy Dreams

I do not mean to imply that all ideals are the cause of psychic pain. Some ideals are life-giving and inspiring. These are the ideals which are noble and yet realistic ideals which lie within the range of our talents and abilities. Such ideals are a gentle spur and motivation toward a beautiful life.

Parents and educators do well when they inspire healthy ideals in their children and students. Ideals like reverence by which the child is motivated to give to every person and every thing the respect and care which is its due. Or the ideal of honesty—truthfulness in speech and gesture, sincerity, straight-forwardness, openness. Or ideals of courtesy, gentleness, fairness. All these ideals lie within the grasp of every person and their attainment adorns one's personality with the graciousness of Jesus.

A truly beautiful ideal is the ideal of *compassion*, the capacity to feel with others their pain and to show them that we care. Compassion for ourselves as well as for others. Gentleness with ourselves, refusing to make unrealistic demands on ourselves, refusing to be unforgiving toward ourselves. Compassion toward others, refusing to judge or to condemn. Feeling the pain of others, understanding, caring, being there for them with support as long as they need us.

A touching example of this kind of compassion was John, the father of Matthew, a young priest who had come for counseling. Matt was an only child and very devoted to his parents. When his mother died a few years after his ordination, it was one of the deepest pains that he had ever experienced. Then, when his dad remarried, Matt's pain of loss became more excruciating. He didn't like his stepmother; he resented her even trying to take his mother's place. So he visited home less and less.

Matt's dad felt his pain. It also hurt him that he did not see Matt more often. So he planned a vacation for the three of them at a resort that they used to go to when Matt's mother was alive. He hoped that the time together at this well-loved resort would help bring the three of them closer together.

Matt went along with the plan mainly to please his dad. When they arrived at the resort, however, a wave of nostalgia overtook him. He excused himself and went to the cottage where they used to stay when his mother was alive. He sat down on the steps, his head in his hands while thoughts from the past came over him like a torrent.

About twenty minutes later his dad came along. He did not say a word at first. He sat down beside Matt, sat there in silence for almost a half-hour. Then he turned to look at Matt, put his arm around Matt's shoulder and said, "I know how you feel, Matt. I understand. I loved her too!" The both of them just sat there and cried, unashamed!

Later on Matt told me that he never felt so touched in his whole life, never felt so understood and accepted.

When he told me the story, I was very touched also. His dad's ability to listen with such sensitivity to Matt's feelings and feel them with evident compassion is one of the most beautiful qualities a human being can have. A less compassionate man could have devastated his son with remarks like: "Come on! Stop this damn self-pity!" Not this father! He was compassionate. Matt told me: "I never loved him so much as I did at that moment."

Another beautiful ideal is the ideal of true humility, that wholesome attractive quality by which a person is absolutely honest about himself. He knows who he is with all his good qualities and all his limitations and he's happy to be just that. He never tries to be anyone else! He wants to be somebody—but the somebody he wants to be is *himself*, his best self, but himself! His desire is to be the best person that he can be within the confines of what he is with his talents and his abilities.

To inspire that kind of dream into the young is to give them the inspiration which puts zest and joy into their lives. It is to give them a possible dream!

Noble ideals, then, attainable ideals, are very healthy. The ideals that cause so much psychic pain are those ideals that are unattainable. "The Impossible Dream" is an attractive song but it is very poor psychology. "Unreachable stars" lead us to nothing but frustration, self-blame, and feelings of inadequacy and helplessness.

Summary

Self-esteem is "the pearl of great price." It is that wholesome, joyful feelings about ourselves which gives us the freedom and the power to unlock all the treasures of our world-system, to live a life that is both successful and loving.

And yet, a healthy self-esteem eludes us unless we also have a healthy and realistic perceptive system. Our perceptions have to be relatively filter-free in order to perceive the true reality of our own beauty and goodness and power.

Just a brief treatment of our perceptive system, however, has revealed how many filters we have which block out this true perception, locked-in filters of all kinds, mobile filters, even everyday misunderstandings and misinterpretations. It might be very easy for us at this point to be discouraged, to feel that the desire for self-esteem is itself "The Impossible Dream!"

Our feelings infallibly follow our perceptions. And our perceptions carry so much garbage from our past life that the realities of our inner and outer world have become twisted and distorted. How can we ever remove that mountain of filters, especially the tenacious, locked-in kind? How can we ever get to see the truth, the truth that will make us free?

The truth is that we have already begun! Just to realize that a large portion of our perceptions comes from *us* rather than from the objective reality is a huge step in the right direction. Maybe half of what we perceive and interpret reflects the real outer world; the other half is our own stuff, our own baggage from our past life.

Just knowing this is such a help because that knowledge will slow us up from making quick judgments; it will motivate us to question our perceptions and to challenge our prejudices, motivate us to clarify and clarify and clarify, until we understand what the other person really means and what he is really like.

In Chapter VII we will consider other positive steps that we can take to reach the truth. But they will be secondary steps. The first and indispensable step is the realization that what seems so clear and evident to us at first sight is not the whole truth! It's colored and distorted and twisted by our own mixed-up baggage. This realization brings humility. And humility takes us half way to the truth.

CHAPTER V

My Special "Guilt Machine": The Reflex to Blame

As we have seen thus far, most of our psychic pain is the direct result of a defective perceptive system. I simply cannot feel good about myself when the standards by which I measure myself are standards that are unattainable—either unattainable for any human being or at least unattainable for this particular human being—myself.

The task of revising our perceptive system is by no means an easy one, but neither is it an impossible one. We will take that up in detail in the last chapter.

Meanwhile it is very important for us to analyze at some length that phenomenon which I feel is the second major cause of psychic pain—and that is our conditioned reflex to blame.

It is evident from just a moment's reflection how much every one of us *dreads* to be blamed. From the small child to the mature adult, the experience of being blamed is an experience of psychic pain. Why? What is the precise feeling that blame triggers off in us that it should be so awfully uncomfortable? It is a feeling of guilt and/or a feeling of inadequacy, both of which are frightful blows to our self-esteem.

There are many ways that you can blame me. You can use words that scold me or a tone of voice that is sharp and angry. You can put on facial expressions which send me a message of distain. In all of these cases, the moment I perceive your signal, I immediately feel guilty or stupid or both!

This is true even if I have not done anything or said anything that is worthy of blame. Unfortunately, I don't *have* to do anything bad to feel that I am bad. I don't have to be stupid to feel stupid! I feel bad the moment I feel the stimulus of your blame. I feel stupid the moment I feel the stimulus of your putting me down!

This feeling reflex to blame is not a natural reflex with which I was born. It is a conditioned reflex, one which I acquired in childhood through the constant correction I experienced from my parents. I was blamed by them whenever I was "bad." So I became *conditioned* to react with a feeling of guilt whenever anyone from that time on would blame me. Being blamed and being bad just seem to go together. Like all reflexes, this conditioned reflex needs neither the intervention of my intellect nor the use of my perceptive system in order to operate. I operate on a stimulus-response basis. The moment the stimulus is given, I automatically feel a response. I don't have to perceive myself as bad before I feel bad and ugly. In the case of blame, I immediately feel ugly and guilty the very moment you blame me!

This fact is what makes the reflex to blame such a frightful source of psychic pain. These ugly feelings of guilt and inadequacy do not necessarily come from any misconduct on my part or from any stupidity or mistakes that I have made. I experience these ugly feelings in exactly the same way that I experience shivering and sweating. Excessive cold will make me shiver whether or not my mind thinks of the cold. In the same way the experience of blame will make me feel ugly and stupid whether or not I have done anything to deserve those feelings.

As a result, it is very difficult for me to detect the insidious action of this reflex and very hard to get relief from the false guilt it causes. As strange as it seems, *real* guilt is much easier to manage. When I feel real guilt I know what I've done wrong and I know what I must do to feel better. But when I feel the neurotic guilt triggered by blame, I don't even know that I feel guilty or stupid! All I know is that I feel rotten and have no idea how I can get to feel better.

This conditioned reflex to blame, therefore, can appropriately be called a "special guilt machine." It "manufactures" guilt in an instant. Worse still, it leaves me confused and bewildered about how to get rid of it.

In order to understand this phenomenon, let's first analyze the nature and effects of all guilt. Then I can distinguish real guilt which is healthy, from neurotic guilt, which is self-destructive. Then we will be in a better position to cope with our reflex to blame.

The Nature and Effects of Guilt

Guilt is that extremely distressful feeling of self-blame in which I look down on myself and despise myself. It is anger at myself for some real or imagined offense that I have committed. It is looking down on myself as unworthy, ugly, bad. Often it is experienced as an absolute disgust for myself! Of its very nature, therefore, guilt diminishes my self-esteem.

We speak of guilt as self-blame and yet in a very true sense guilt is blame from my parents, my parents whose values and ideals I have internalized to that point that they are now a part of myself. My parents' ideals and values are now part of my perceptive system in the form of locked-in filters.

This process of internalization became so complete by the time I was a young adult, that now I can no longer distinguish the "pointing finger" of blame as coming from my parents. The pointing finger is really from my parents but now I experience it as coming from myself. Let me explain.

When I was a baby, I had absolutely no idea of who I was or what I was worth. Except for some very primitive instincts, all my perceptions, values and ways of acting had to be learned. And, of course, my most powerful teachers were my parents.

In a very real sense my parents actually defined me. It was they who told me my meaning and my worth or my lack of worth. I not only depended on them for food and warmth, for shelter and protection! I also depended on them for love, affection, and approval. If they gave me these things, I was happy and content because I felt that I was really somebody worthwhile! If they deprived me of these things, or gave them to me grudgingly, then I was miserable. I felt that I was really a pest, of no real worth!

Therefore, the task of pleasing these two powerful "giants," the task of getting them to affirm me, became the all important business of my life. I not only needed them in order to stay alive physically. I needed their approval and affirmation in order to stay alive emotionally, to feel good about myself. My whole sense of self was in their hands. They had the power to affirm me or to crush me.

Praise from them in any form, a hug, a kiss, approving words, a smile, brightened up my life, told me that I was good and lovable. Their praise for my efforts at play or in school told me that I was adequate. Their letting me make some small choices, and at adolescence, their allowing me to rebel a bit and shout out my "Hey, I'm me!" without too much fuss and with no denial of love—all that told me that I do have power, the power to pull my own strings, and the right to do so!

Blame from them in any form, a scowl, cold silence, ignoring me, yelling at me, hitting me, made me feel miserable. I was not only deprived of their love, which meant a lot to me, but I was now also impoverished in my own love for myself. I felt worthless, bad, ugly— guilty.

During my very early years, my parents had this power over me only when they were physically present to me. When they told me not to take any more jelly beans and they were present, I didn't take any jelly beans! I needed their approval. I needed to avoid their anger and disdain. But when they were not present, I'd take all the jelly beans I wanted.

Around the age of five or six, however, I began to incorporate my parents within myself. The mouth is the reality tester for the child. Things get evaluated by how they taste. Well, in somewhat an analogous fashion, I "swallowed" my mother and father. I took them inside me so to speak. I took inside myself and made my own [in the form of locked-in perceptions] their values, their attitudes, their prejudices—almost their entire perceptive system. If unshined shoes were "disgraceful" in my mother's eyes, then unshined shoes were "disgraceful" in my eyes. If my father detested boys who could not play ball, then athletes were the only real boys for me also. And, if I discovered that I was not a good athlete, then I did not feel like a real boy at all. I felt that I was a sissy. I felt inadequate. I felt guilty.

From the age of five or six, therefore, and throughout the rest of my life, my parents and their value system, their perceptive system, have been inside of me, and are really a part of me now.

For years, the sight of a woman smoking a cigarette used to bother me. I was uncomfortable in her presence and felt inclined to think less of her. The fact that I had such an attitude bothered me terribly. I felt ashamed of feeling this way. In my mind I knew that it was a prejudice. Then one day, when my brothers and sisters were relating how much my mother looked down on women who smoked, I realized where I learned my prejudice. Smoking women were "hussies" to her, so, like it or not, they were "hussies" to me. And it took me years to lessen the impact of that prejudice.

My parents did not die with their physical death! As far as I am concerned, they still go on living inside of me. And so, at least from early adolescence onward, my parents did not have to be physically present to me in order to exercise their power over me. They exercise their control now from inside me.

So, whenever I do anything or say anything which is against their value system, I immediately sense their finger pointing at me with disdain and blame. I feel guilty, even if what I did or said was not objectively evil or destructive.

This feeling isn't even limited to my words and actions. Even when I feel something which my parents "despised," such as feelings of sexual arousal, anger, jealousy, etc., immediately from within myself they point the finger of guilt at me and say: "You're a disgrace! You're no good!" It makes no difference that my anger and jealousy came upon me unbidden, that they are not my fault! That does not matter; the finger of guilt still points at me and I feel ugly and bad. In my mind I know that I can't help these feelings. No matter! In my feelings I feel unworthy and guilty.

The Effects of Guilt

There are two devastating effects that follow from my feelings of guilt. The first is a loss of self-esteem, sometimes to the point of actual self-contempt. The second is an unconscious but insistent urge to *atone* for my "evil doings" by inflicting some punishment upon myself.

My internalized parents retain their power to tell me that I am bad whenever I do anything or even *feel* anything that is displeasing to them. From within me they convince me that I am ugly—a disgrace! Depression follows me immediately.

It is this awful feeling of depression that leads me to the second effect of guilt—the powerful, insistent urge to make reparation for my "faults" by punishing myself.

This is the hardest part of the guilt-syndrome for most of us to understand. Our life force is so strong, our desire for happiness so all-embracing, that it seems incongruous that we would want to cause ourselves pain! Actually, my ultimate purpose in punishing myself this way is not to feel pain; my ultimate goal is to feel better about myself. The pain I cause myself is really a tool that I use to ease the greater pain of self-hatred.

I have no other avenue of escape! If you look down on me, I can find some direct relief. I can tell myself: "He just doesn't understand me. My motives were good!" But when I look down on myself, when *I* feel ugly, then I have no avenue of escape except to punish myself, to atone for my "evil." My real purpose, of course, is not to feel more pain; my real goal is to offer the pain I cause myself as a *substitute* for the greater pain, the excruciating pain of despising myself. It is really a "bribe" offered to my internalized parents.

The Ways That I Punish Myself

I usually arrange my punishment in two ways: First, by refusing to accept love or affirmation; and second, by actively arranging for myself to get injured or hurt.

Once I feel plagued by guilt feelings, I cannot easily allow love to touch me. The reason is this: I'm convinced that I am bad. But when you express love for me, your love tells me that I am good. How can I let you tell me that! If I accept your message that I am good, I'd feel like a hypocrite! I'd feel like a liar, pretending to be something that I am not. All this would only make me feel worse about myself. I was bad before but now I'd be a hypocrite as well!

Imagine how you would feel, for example, if someone affirmed you by saying that you were a world-renowned pianist, when you know that you can hardly manage to play "Chopsticks." The compliment may be well-intentioned but it is next to impossible for you to enjoy it because you know that it just isn't true. So you cannot let yourself pretend that it is true. You'd feel like a complete phony!

Besides, someone might ask you to sit down and play the piano, and you'd be embarrassed to tears.

When I feel guilty, I have the same need to push love away from myself. Accepting love and affection would only make me feel more guilty and increase my pain. So, I have to deny all compliments. I have to pull back from all affection. I have to steel myself from feeling your love.

This isn't a case of my not needing your love and affirmation! I need your love desperately, especially now when I feel so rotten about myself, but I simply cannot let your love touch me or warm me. The pathway for the guilty person is a lonely path. I simply cannot allow a loved one to walk it with me!

The second way I punish myself is by arranging for punishment of some kind. Often I do this by disparaging myself. I tell you: "Oh, you shouldn't listen to me! You know how stupid I am! I always get things backward!" Or I laugh at myself when I give an opinion as though my opinion makes no sense. Sometimes I dress in a way that makes me look sloppy or laughable. Or I make very obvious mistakes, so obvious that others will think that I am quite limited mentally.

Many times the punishment is in the form of an accident in which I am injured. Unconsciously, I set myself up to be hurt.

Often, the punishment takes the form of not allowing myself any real joy or pleasure. I don't let myself relax in my spare time. I do some work instead. I don't let myself enjoy a drink or a nice meal. I just take anything that's available, even if it is cold. That's good enough for someone like me! I get up early when there is no need to do so. I don't share my pains or hurts with empathetic friends. I just treat myself shabbily!

I worked with two young women years ago, natural sisters, who spent every weekend visiting the sick and lonely in a huge city hospital. The poor whom they cared for were very touched by their exquisite kindness. They would bring little gift items, especially at holiday time, write letters for those who found it difficult to write by themselves. Mostly, they would sit and listen to the pain, the fears, the loneliness, and show by their words and tone of voice and facial expressions that they understood, that they appreciated the pain.

The services they rendered were really beautiful, except for one thing. Their generosity was not just an act of love; it was in large part an act of un-doing, an act of self-punishment. They both felt so guilty about some things that had happened in their family life that they felt driven to atone and to make reparation. So, even though they worked hard from Monday to Friday in the business world, they hardly allowed themselves a single weekend to relax. It was very sad! Their goodness to the poor would have been so much more beautiful if they could also have been a little good to themselves.

Another rather poignant example is that of Mark, a forty-five year old bachelor. Through no fault of his own, Mark is a homosexual. The knowledge of his sexual orientation was somewhat forced on him when he became aroused on a camping trip as a teenager. There were no sexual actions. The other young man didn't even realize what Mark was feeling. Nevertheless, from that day to the present, Mark has not only struggled to suppress all awareness of his homosexuality, but he has consistently punished himself for that orientation.

He has allowed himself to become grossly overweight. He hates himself for this but will do nothing to change his eating habits. He likewise has practically cut himself off from the comfort that can come from friendship and warm human interchange. Except for an occasional visit to his sister, he reaches out to no one and discourages anyone from reaching out to him. Partly this isolation is caused by his fear that others might discover his terribly dark secret if he allowed them to get close to him. Mostly, his self-imposed loneliness is a self-punishment, an undoing for his "ugliness" in being homosexual.

An Important Distinction

All guilt is painful. All guilt is an attack upon my self-esteem. Not all guilt, however, is unhealthy! There is a type of guilt which is realistic and necessary in order to keep me from destructive behavior and to preserve me as a socialized responsible and mature individual. Before we discuss in detail our conditioned reflex to guilt — a reflex which generates neurotic guilt, it is important for us to distinguish neurotic guilt from this real and healthy guilt.

Real guilt, mature guilt, is that painful feeling of self-blame which I feel when I have knowingly and willfully done something that is morally wrong. It is anger at myself because I deliberately did something that was *destructive*—either for myself or for others. I told a vicious lie. I gave in to my jealousy and spoke to you in a sarcastic and hurting way. I satisfied my longing to gossip and revealed secrets about you to others. I gave full vent to my anger and stabbed you with a knife. I defrauded you of your life's savings through a deceitful business arrangement. In all these cases, I should feel guilty because I did do something wrong. I should be angry at myself, the same as I would be angry at others if they acted in a similar way. My conduct was immoral and unsocialized; I should feel responsible and guilty!

Guilt in these cases of objectively immoral behavior is healthy—even though I feel for the time being the psychic pain of self-blame and the powerful urge to undo the wrong that I have committed. It is just and fair that I feel that pain. It is appropriate that I try to undo the effects of my behavior because my behavior was unjust. The scales of fairness were unbalanced! It is therefore a healthy sign of maturity and responsibility on my part to feel pressured to balance them, to acknowledge to you that I was unfair to you and to tell you that I am deeply sorry, to repay you in some way for the damages that I have caused you.

Real guilt is healthy also because once I have acknowledged my wrong-doing and made atonement, I can let my guilt subside. I no longer blame myself. I can forgive myself and let myself feel peace and a renewed self-esteem. I was wrong, but I'm not wrong now! I'm no longer a sinner; I used to be one!

This is a true sign of real and healthy guilt as distinguished from neurotic guilt, the fact that I can let the guilt feeling go the moment I repent and pay back. I know that God has forgiven me and I can accept His forgiveness with deep gratitude.

Whenever I am not able to forgive myself in this manner, then that is a sure sign that some neurotic guilt is mixed in with the healthy guilt. It means that my perfectionistic filter is still firmly in place. My need to be perfect makes me absolutely merciless in my self-condemnation now that I have made the mistake of sinning. Healthy guilt does not have such a filter. Healthy guilt knows that I am a creature, that I can make mistakes. But, once I have repented of my mistakes, it is no longer a present mistake. It is a thing of the past. I've paid back. I've atoned. And I can welcome God's gracious mercy and rejoice in it.

Neurotic guilt cannot let me forgive myself. In neurotic guilt my sin was not only against God! In neurotic guilt, I've destroyed my "idealized self." I've desecrated the "shrine" of my exalted, unrealistic image that I am a superior being. Other people are just ordinary, so I can forgive them for committing sins and making mistakes, but in no way can I forgive this "superhuman" person—myself. The shrine of my superior holiness and perfection has been desecrated by me. I can never again imagine that I am perfect. How can I possibly forgive myself for such a "sacrilege"!

Finally, healthy guilt, though painful, is a blessing for myself and for society because it acts as a deterrent against antisocial and destructive behavior. It is the best kind of deterrent—an *inner brake*, so to speak, to motivate me and hold me back from sin. Without such an inner deterrent, I would be a psychopath, a wildly destructive person whose only restraint is his fear of punishment from without, his fear of arrest and imprisonment.

A psychopath has a seriously impaired guilt system. He could cut a person's throat for no reason and smile as the person gasped for breath and bled to death. He has little if any feelings for others or for their pain. And so it means very little to him if he hurts others. He feels little or no guilt or remorse. Such a person is terribly sick—and terribly dangerous. His only deterrent is his fear of external punishment. He is just like a run-away truck racing down a hill with no brakes. It can only be stopped from without. The driver's only hope is to steer it toward an upward grade where the force of gravity will gradually slow it down. However, its potential for destruction is easily imagined. Psychopaths have the same potential. They have to be locked up in special prisons and very carefully guarded.

Narcissism: A Diminished Sense of Guilt

Our capacity to feel real guilt, therefore, is a sign of health and maturity. In fact, probably one of the most serious ailments in our society is the loss of this sense of guilt. Both psychotherapists and theologians are deeply concerned about the fearful increase in our times of narcissism—that ugly mental syndrome in which a person's whole life and feelings are centered only in himself.

The narcissist has a greatly diminished sense of guilt because other people and their rights mean very little to him. *He* is the only one that matters. Everyone else is only there to serve him and his needs. Only his feelings count, only his plans and his desires—no one else's! And so, if others get stepped on or injured as he pursues his own ends, that causes him no pain. He probably does not even notice their discomfort.

If something feels good to him, then it's okay—no matter who else gets hurt or injured. If something is hard for him, then why should he push himself! It does not matter that others are inconvenienced.

The narcissist doesn't even have to justify himself. He doesn't have to say, "Other people's feelings don't really matter!" He's hardly even aware that other people can have hurt feelings. He is so self-centered that the pains and joys of others hardly enter his consciousness. His world begins and ends with himself.

The Age of Narcissism

One of the tragedies of our age is that narcissism seems to be on the increase. Perhaps it is one of the products of the "Me" generation. Perhaps it is the result of a diminished sense of sinfulness. These may be contributing factors. In my own mind, however, I think it is due most of all to an *impoverished sense of true self-worth*.

Once I realize my true worth and dignity as a person, I automatically put a *high value* on what I do and on what I say. I realize that my actions and words have the power to touch people deeply, either for pain or for joy. As a result, I become very careful not to use my words or actions carelessly. I become very sensitive not to hurt or bruise others.

It is much different when I have very little esteem for myself. Then I feel that my words and actions are not of the *minutest importance* to others. I can't believe that what I say could possibly bring others joy. Who am I! No one notices me! No one really gives a damn whether I live or die! So how could I possibly touch them! I no longer feel any responsibility.

This is the tragedy, not only for the narcissist himself but for

the people around him, especially those who want to relate to him
and have him care for them in return.

Edward, for example, was a priest in his mid-thirties. He was
referred to the Center by his major superior because "frankly, he's
driving the rest of us out of our mind!" Edward was a narcissist. He
lived his life in the monastery as though *no one else lived there.* He
took any car, any time, without ever bothering to sign it out. He
performed many, many marriages and never entered the records of
them into the Church books nor sent any notice to City Hall for
civil records. Unbelievable confusion and inconvenience resulted,
both for the couples themselves and for the other priests who had to
go searching out the facts and get the sworn testimony of witnesses
in order to straighten out the records.

If Edward were repentant about all this trouble he caused, that
feeling would have been realistic guilt and a sign of health. However, he was in no way repentant! He hardly even adverted to the
fact that others suffered because of his carelessness.

His performance in group process at our Center was somewhat
the same. He hardly even heard what the others in the group revealed about themselves and their feelings. He would cut others off
in the middle of a sentence to come out with something entirely
unrelated to what they had been saying. It wasn't meanness on his
part. He didn't intend to hurt the persons he cut off. He hadn't
been listening to what they were saying. Worse still, he didn't even
seem to notice that they were talking. His world began and ended
with himself!

When the members of the group confronted him on this insensitivity, he said that he was sorry, but I could tell from the way he
responded that he hardly knew what they were talking about. Saying that he was sorry was the easiest way to blunt their "complaint"
and extricate himself from his "messy situation." It took well over a
year before some ray of insight finally touched Edward. One day in
his private session he said with an appropriate tone of sadness: "Jim,
I realize that I don't have a friend in the world. I've just made
believe that I've had a lot of people who care about me. I don't think
there is *anyone* who does!" And he started to cry. I was touched and
very happy! "Ed," I said, "I appreciate your pain, but I can't tell
you how good I feel that you miss real closeness. You're on your
way!"

His pain was soon followed by a deeper understanding of *why* he didn't make real friends, as well as insight into the destructive behavior patterns which alienated people from him. In time he became more responsible for his words and actions, began to believe that he had the power to please others and the power to hurt them. And now when he did hurt others, he felt a sense of guilt, good, healthy, mature guilt.

The ability to experience real guilt, therefore, is a sign of health and maturity. It shows that this person *values himself* and assumes responsibility for his words and his actions.

Neurotic Guilt

Far different from real guilt is neurotic guilt. In neurotic guilt I feel the same painfully distressing feeling of self-blame as I do in real guilt, except now I have not done anything to deserve that feeling. I look down on myself in neurotic guilt, many times to the point of real disdain and disgust and yet I have done nothing to deserve this awful feeling. Neurotic guilt feelings, therefore, are inappropriate feelings because there is no valid objective reason for my feeling this way.

As in the case of real guilt I also experience a strong impulse to undo the "wrong" by punishing myself. I cannot let love touch me, cannot enjoy compliments or affection—and I set myself up to be punished by making disparaging remarks about myself. I actually punish myself by not allowing myself any pleasure or joy.

The tragic part about neurotic guilt is that I go through this painful "undoing" process even though there is no misconduct to undo. And perhaps, most unfairly of all, the majority of times I don't even know what is happening to me. I don't know that I am blaming myself. I don't know that I'm arranging to punish myself. All I know is that I feel terribly depressed—and I don't know why.

I don't even suspect that my painful feelings are guilt feelings because I know I didn't do anything morally wrong. So I don't expect to have guilt feelings. Why should I be blaming myself when I haven't done anything wrong! So when I feel the ugly depression, I have no idea (most often) that my feelings are feelings of guilt and self-blame. I don't know why I'm depressed and I set about searching in my mind and heart for some cause on which I can hang this ugly feeling.

These two characteristics are the principal ways in which neurotic guilt is different from real guilt, namely: 1) I have not done anything morally wrong to trigger off guilt feelings; 2) Most often I am not aware that my painful depression is due to feelings of guilt. I just know that I feel awful and keep searching for some reason why I feel that way. The following diagram may make this more clear.

Diagram 7.

1st	I deliberately do something which is morally *wrong*	*1st*	I feel depressed (guilty)
	↓		↓
2nd	I feel guilty.	*2nd*	I search to find the cause of my depression *"What did I do?"*

In real guilt my morally offensive conduct comes first in time and then my guilt feelings come second—caused by my immoral conduct. In neurotic guilt, however, there is no immoral conduct to cause the guilt feelings. Here, the ugly feelings come first and then my mind goes searching for some explanation for those feelings. I ask myself: "Why do I feel this way? What did I do to make me feel so badly!"

Because I don't usually recognize these ugly feelings as guilt feelings, the "undoing process" becomes a prolonged process, precisely because there is no immoral conduct for me to take back and regret.

In real guilt I can ask God and my neighbor for forgiveness. And then I can forgive myself. Once I do that the undoing process is all but finished. In neurotic guilt, however, relief is not so easy to attain. I have not done anything wrong. I don't have any immoral conduct to repent. I don't even know that I feel guilty! So the painful undoing process drags on and on. I keep pushing love away from me. I keep arranging to look foolish. I keep holding myself back from ordinary joys and pleasures. It's so ironical that it is easier for me to experience forgiveness and peace when I have knowingly done something wrong than it is when I have neurotic guilt and have not done anything wrong at all!

Cases of Neurotic Guilt

It's only natural then to ask "Why do I feel depressed and uncomfortable if I have not done anything morally wrong? Where do the guilty feelings come from?" This is *the* important question.

There are two big sources of neurotic guilt feelings. The first we have analyzed at considerable length in the fourth chapter, i.e., our distorted perception by which we measure our words and actions and even our feelings by unrealistic standards and unattainable ideals. When we do this, we are bound to feel guilty and inadequate each time we fail to live up to these unrealistic "demands." So, for example, if my locked-in perception sees all anger as ugly and bad, then every time I feel angry, I automatically feel guilty, even though I am not responsible for starting my angry feelings. I can't help but feel angry at times. You hurt me—or I think that you hurt me—and immediately I feel the response of anger,—I feel like hurting you back.

These angry feelings are not bad. God made me to respond to hurt by having angry feelings. My angry feelings become bad only if I act them out in a destructive way, i.e., if I attack you or hurt myself. But, since my filter sees all angry feelings as bad in themselves, then as soon as I feel angry I also feel guilty and depressed.

The same is true for all my other distorted filters. If I have an "all-or-nothing" filter, then I am bound to suffer neurotic guilt feelings any time that the job I do is not done perfectly. If it's not all-perfect, then my filter lets me see it as a failure and in my feelings, I feel inadequate and stupid.

Our distorted perceptive system, therefore, is the source of most of our psychic pain. From these distortions flow most of our feelings of guilt as well as our feelings of inferiority and helplessness. In the next chapter we'll try to deal with the problem of correcting these distorted perceptions.

The Reflex to Blame

The second most powerful source of guilt feelings is our *conditioned reflex to blame*. It is very important for us to understand the exact nature of this reflex, to identify the various forms that blame can take and finally to discover how we can ward off the destructive guilt feelings which it causes.

A reflex is a spontaneous response to a stimulus. Shine a flashlight into my eye and immediately the pupil in my eye will contract. There is no need for my mind to make that decision. My automatic nervous system takes care of it. The stimulus itself, the light, triggers the response, the contraction of my pupil. This kind of reflex is a natural reflex.

Other types of reflexes are learned through the conditioning process of constant repetition. So, for example, when I first learn to drive a car, my mind has to command my leg to step on the brake at a red light. But, after I do this many times, the brain, as a clever executive, gives over the task to my automatic nervous system, and it now becomes a reflex. Now my foot automatically steps on the brake as soon as I see the red light. My foot has been so conditioned by repetition that now I have developed a conditioned reflex.

Well, our early childhood training, by praise and blame, has created in us a conditioned reflex to praise and blame. We were praised so often for being good and blamed so often for being bad that we now automatically associate praise with being a good person and blame with being a bad person. Praise and blame now automatically trigger off in me their associated feelings.

I don't have to be aware of doing anything good. Any sign of praise, a smile, a hug, a word of commendation, triggers off a nice, warm feeling in me. The same with blame. I don't have to be consciously aware of doing anything morally wrong. *Any sign of blame*—a scowl, a put-down, sullen silence, etc., triggers off in me an ugly feeling of guilt and inferiority. My brain doesn't enter into it. I can feel guilty and inferior even though I have done absolutely nothing to warrant those feelings.

It's sad to note that for most people the conditioned reflex to praise is not as powerful as the reflex to blame. The one exception to this is the person who has a highly developed self-esteem. He already has many good feelings about himself, so why shouldn't other people notice his goodness and praise him for it. "Thank you very much!" Most of us, however, do not have such an exalted feeling of self-worth. So we are very suspicious of praise. But when we are blamed, we buy the ugly feelings "hook, line, and sinker."

Hence, the signs of praise and affirmation have to be given very subtly and with a delicate finesse. As we'll see later on in the last chapter, nice feelings about ourselves can only enter in and improve our self-image through a very narrow channel.

The Multiple Faces of Blame

Since it is blame in any form that sets my special guilt-machine into motion, I must try to identify the various types of blame. Then I will become more conscious of my neurotic guilt feelings, more adept at naming them for what they are, and finally have more skill in refusing to "buy" guilt when I have done nothing to merit guilt. This is the ultimate freedom, when I "turn around" my guilt-machine so that its darts no longer sting me.

A marvelous example of this type of maturity, this wonderful freedom of not buying guilt when it is not deserved, was St. Thomas More. Thomas More knew in his conscience that he could not take the oath of supremacy which affirmed that the king was the only head on earth of the Church in England. So he refused to take it, refused in spite of the overwhelming blame that he had to face, blame from the king, criticism from the lords and nobles, and, worst of all, the painful blame from his wife and daughter.

His daughter, Meg, was extremely dear to him. He loved her keen mind, very much like his own, and cherished her goodness. Meg used every argument she could think of to get him to recognize Henry as head of the Church in England, all to no avail. Then, shortly before his death, Meg pulled out all the "stops." She heaped blame on him. Told him that he was selfish, proud, arrogant. After all, Bishops had taken the oath. Who did he think he was! He could not possibly love his wife or herself, and just willingly go to his death!

Any lesser man would have been so tortured by neurotic guilt from all this blame that he would have used rationalization and justified taking the oath to Henry as head of the Church of England. But not Thomas More! He knew that he was following his conscience, that he was *good* and not selfish or proud. So there were no ugly feelings of depression and self-blame. He said to Meg: "Meg, all men die sooner or later. The lucky ones are those who die for love. Meg, I'm one of the lucky ones —I'm dying for love!" And his peace was so real that he was able to jest with the executioner just before he was beheaded. He lifted his beard and said with a smile: "The beard didn't commit treason!"

Thomas More was not only a great saint, he was a shining example of our human ability to reverse our "guilt-machine" and recondition our conditioned reflex to blame. Once we do that, the highway to peace and freedom and maturity is wide open. Then no longer will neurotic guilt "make cowards of us all!"

First, however, we have to be able to identify the various faces of blame, i.e., the many ways in which we can *feel* blamed and therefore feel the pain of neurotic guilt. There are three kinds of signals that our feelings interpret as blame: actual blame, implied blame and unreasonable expectations and demands from others.

1. Actual Blame

Actual blame is an intentional and conscious accusation on my part that you are bad or stupid or both. Here, I don't simply say that I disagree with the way you think or the way you acted, I actually attribute moral guilt or stupidity to you. "You had no damn right to use the gym last night! It's a mess and my committee has no chance to decorate it for tonight." I'm saying that you're selfish and inconsiderate. Even though you had every right to use the gym in your mind and you know that you had that right, nevertheless, in your feelings, you feel bad and ugly. My blame triggered your guilt feelings.

Or I say in response to your opinion about our American involvement in Central America: "That's the dumbest thing I've ever heard!" You may get furious—understandably so. You may attempt to show me that there are very good reasons for your opinion, *but* in your *feelings* you have that disturbing feeling that you are *inadequate*. It was triggered off by my insensitive and unjustified blame.

It's regrettable how often this kind of blame occurs in religious life and the priesthood. In some rectories and convents "put-downs" like this are common fare. It's a terrible lack of reverence for the dignity of other persons. Even more, its an attack on their self-esteem because it sets the guilt-machine in full motion.

Jack, for example, was a very bright and articulate young priest who had learned to use his verbal ability as an instrument of power. A Sherman tank would have been less destructive. Whenever the pastor gave a directive, Jack would subject it to the most devastating kind of ridicule, using half-truths to reinforce his arguments. The pastor, a gentle man, was no match for Jack in this verbal battle. Jack made the directives seem contradictory and childish. The pastor felt stupid, inadequate, confused. He became more and more tongue-tied and gradually held back altogether from giving directives or even making suggestions. To all extents and purposes, Jack became the pastor and the poor old man just sank more and more into a state of apathy and depression. His self-esteem had been devastated by the darts of Jack's ridicule.

2. Implied Blame

It is not only *actual* blame in the form of blaming words or accusations of stupidity that can set our guilt machine in motion. We can cause those same painful feelings in others even when our blame is only *implied*. The truth is that we have a whole array of signals by which we can express our displeasure for others or cast blame on them.

We can use a tone of voice, which *reeks* with disapproval and disrespect. We can present facial expressions that just broadcast our utter disdain! Our arsenal is replete both with actions and with calculated omissions that can wither other people. We can use withdrawal and coldness to put others in a "deep freeze." We can use silence, a sullen silence, to imply that they are bad or stupid. We can withhold eye-contact, refuse to recognize their presence and by negative body language, turn away from them and turn them off.

All these signals are powerful expressions of implied blame. And merely that implication of blame is enough to set in motion another's guilt machine—with all those ugly consequences of guilt, depression, diminished self-esteem, the confused search to understand why and the powerful urge to undo, to set things right by punishing themselves.

Years ago, the Superior of a large convent used sullen silence and withdrawal with alarming effectiveness on her Sisters. Whenever she was displeased with the conduct or performance of any Sister, she would stop talking to everyone, put on a long face and effectively isolate herself from the whole community.

The reaction among the Sisters was a general feeling of uneasiness and guilt, followed by the usual search for meaning. "What's wrong? What did we do?" They found themselves talking in whispers and tip-toeing around the convent as though somehow they had done something wrong and now they should undo it by being very silent and unobtrusive.

The Superior's action was terribly manipulative and cruel. The point here, however, is this—what made her maneuver so powerful was the painful feelings of guilt which she engendered in all the Sisters by her strong implication of blame. That implication set their guilt machine in high gear. They felt guilty—even though they had done nothing to merit that feeling.

Foremost among these signals of implied blame is the excruciatingly painful signal of *laughing* at another person. There are few things that can strike at the heart of a person's self-esteem as quickly as this can. I suppose this is because most of us would rather consider ourselves to be bad than to consider ourselves to be stupid. That feeling is almost unbearable.

When someone laughs at me, he may not be using the word "stupid," but his laughter *implies* that my actions or my comments are so incongruous, so far from making sense, that they are laughable. Such an implication may be absolutely wrong. It may be this person himself who is the inadequate one, unable to understand what I have said. No matter! The intellect doesn't enter into this process. My guilt-machine by-passes the brain. Just the fact that the implication of my stupidity has been made through his laughter, just *that* triggers off in me feelings of inadequacy and stupidity, feelings so painful that I'd almost do anything to prevent them from happening.

It is really tragic that this happens in religious life and the priesthood—more tragic that it happens so often! In fairness to priests and religious, I think that most often this is not done intentionally. Very few of us start out to cause pain in others. Most often we just don't appreciate at the moment of our laughter what painful consequences our laughter can have.

Something strikes us funny. Something in the other person's remarks or actions comes across as incongruous, unfitting, out-of-place, and we laugh. That's it! Nothing more! We make no conclusion that this other person is stupid. We have absolutely no intention of implying as much! What he said simply struck us as funny.

However, just that signal of laughing at him almost always acts as a triggering mechanism for his guilt-machine, and he *feels* stupid even though we had no intention of implying that he is stupid.

Knowing all this can be a helpful tool for me. It can make me much more sensitive to the feelings of others, much more careful not to hurt. It can also help me to be more self-possessed when it is myself who is the victim of guilt-implying signals. I can say to myself: "Hey wait a minute! *I'm* not stupid because that person is insensitive! There's a problem all right, but it is his!"

3. Unreasonable Expectations and Demands

The final set of signals which activate my guilt-machine are those series of unreasonable expectations and unfair demands which others put upon me. Others have *their* ideas about how I should be and how I should act—and *God help me if I don't live up completely to their agenda for me! When I fail to comply with their program for me, they punish me with blame*, actual or implied.

Sometimes others will endow me with expectations of perfection. They may love me and admire me, but their love is conditional. It is given in full only when my performance is perfect. If I get 90% on my exam instead of 100%, they are surprised and shocked. Strong disapproval is written all over their face. "What happened! Surely you can do better than that!" My feelings regretfully see this signal as *blame*. So, instead of being able to rejoice over my 90%, I feel guilty and inadequate that I didn't do better.

If I've attended every community meeting this year but am unable to go to this one, you are visibly disappointed and let down. You can't quite understand why. You really expected more of me.—You may mean well. You may even feel that you are complimenting me by implying that I have an unusually fine loyalty to community. But my feelings don't hear it that way. My feelings hear it as *blame* and they react with discomfort and guilt.

Perfectionistic parents constantly put unrealistic expectations upon their children. It may be in an area of marks. It may be in sports. It may even be in the area of feelings. Their children should never feel angry or frustrated or sexually aroused. In some cases their children shouldn't even *cry*, even though crying is a wholesome, healthy release of deep and pent-up feelings. Consequently their children feel *constantly blamed*, constantly guilty and inadequate. And they develop locked-in perceptions of perfectionistic expectations of themselves which haunt them with guilt throughout their life.

It's important for me to check out my own attitudes in this regard. If my conversation is full of words like "should" and "should not," I may be putting a lot of unfair demands on those around me.

Sometimes, of course, these words *do* apply. The fact that we have rights automatically implies that we also have obligations— "should" and "should nots." If you have a right to your reputation, and you do!, then I have an obligation not to reveal things that will destroy your reputation. There *are* some definite "shoulds" and "should nots" in life just as there are some guilt feelings that are healthy.

All too often, however, the "shoulds" that we impose on other people (and on ourselves!) are not really true obligations. They are unrealistic demands and unwarranted expectations flowing from neurotic and imagined perceptions of how things "ought to be." And almost automatically they create psychic pain of guilt or inadequacy. It's important that we never say "should" either to ourselves or to others unless we are talking about a genuine obligation!

Sometimes the demand that we experience is the demand for one hundred percent attention and love; a demand which cannot be met, even by the most loving and generous of mothers.

Mary, for example, had a friend, Cathy, who wanted Mary entirely for herself. She wanted all of her free time, all of her attention. As long as Mary made every effort to meet those demands, their relationship went along somewhat smoothly. However, whenever Mary gave some attention to her other friends,

Cathy would be tortured by jealousy and blame Mary for her "self-ishness and lack of sensitivity." She'd cry and scream at Mary: "You don't love me! You're no friend!"

All of these outbursts caused Mary great discomfort. She found herself trying to remove her guilty feelings by constantly reassuring Cathy that she loved her. She even pulled back from her other friends and found herself uneasy whenever her other friends would greet her or affirm her. Instead of enjoying such marks of affection, she dreaded them because she feared that Cathy would see them and react with another outburst.

Mary's pain was the pain of neurotic guilt. It made no difference to her feelings that she was actually being a good and a mature person in allowing these other friends into her life. She wasn't able to enjoy their company nor her own wholesomeness in being open to love and friendship, because her reflex to blame made her feel tortured with neurotic guilt feelings. She found herself saying: "I'm hurting Cathy! She has suffered so much pain in her life and now I'm adding to it!" She found herself attempting to ease this guilt by "making things up to Cathy" by showing Cathy even more attention.

It was only after months in counseling that Mary was able to recognize her painful feelings as *guilt* feelings. Then gradually she was able to see that she was not the cause of Cathy's pain (the true cause was deep in Cathy's past, in her lack of qualitative mothering, a mothering which part of her was still seeking). She began to see also that neither she nor anyone else could possibly fulfill Cathy's insatiable "needs," that it was *Cathy* who had to change! It was Cathy who had to re-assess her "needs" and make them more realistic. Mary finally saw that the best way for her to help Cathy was to be true to herself and to her other friends.

Another way in which the expectation of a hundred percent love can be expressed is in the demand for perfect understanding and empathy. And this demand can be made even when the demanding person expresses his feelings so poorly and with such mixed signals that no one could understand that he is in pain. He feels lonely, for example, and has a strong need to talk about his feelings with an understanding friend. But he doesn't say that. Instead he bursts into the community room with a happy-go-lucky swagger and a big smile and announces: "Anyone going out for a walk?" No one takes him up on the walk because no one has even the slightest clue that he is lonely and hurt.

In *his* mind, however, it makes no difference that he gave such poor signals. He complains to you later: "A real friend should be able to sense what his friend is going through whether it is expressed or not!"

That expectation is so unrealistic! Maybe once or twice in our lifetime we may have a friend who is so sensitive and intuitive that he can read even the faintest signals and understand our feelings before we actually express them, a friend who notices that faintest change in our facial muscles, the smallest difference in our breathing, the slightest hint of weariness or tension! Such a friend is an unspeakable gift! However, that kind of exquisite sensitivity is very rare! It is unfair for us to "demand" that from our friends or to punish them with guilt feelings when they are not able to be so intuitive.

Each of us longs to be understood by our friends. That desire is perfectly human and understandable. But it's only fair that we give our friends a chance to understand us. Each of us has the "tools" to communicate our ideas and feelings with accurate words and appropriate effect.

I could say to my friend: "Joe, I feel awfully depressed today. I don't even know why. I really need you to help me sort it all out!" *Then* my friend has a "fighting chance" to understand me and be there with me. But to expect my friends to read my mind or look into my heart is an unrealistic expectation.

One could give many examples of unfair expectations and demands. A whole book wouldn't be sufficient to discuss them all. But perhaps we can consider one more example of the more common type of demands, and that is the expectation I can have that others "should" think my way, "should" feel the way I do and "should" act as I suppose that they should.

This happens most often in those dependent type of relationships where the one partner seems to "take charge" of the other partner's life. In such relationships, both are dependent because both live in dread of being rejected by the other. The dominant partner handles this anxiety by completely controlling his friend. His friend has to think his way and act his way. His friend has to love golf because he loves it; has to hate movies because he hates them. His rationale is: "When I have my friend all tied up this way, he won't be able to abandon me!"

The partner who is obviously dependent copes with his anxiety by thus allowing himself to be controlled. It is just the other side of the coin. He feels that his constant compliance will so please his partner that his partner will never reject him. Dependent relationships are almost always guilt-ridden because of these unrealistic expectations.

This kind of demand, however, be it implicit or explicit, can occur even in more healthy relationships. I suspect that the root cause of this is the locked-in perception of "all-or-nothing." If you don't think my way, then you are not simply being your own person, you are taking a stand against me. Not true, of course. But once I see it that way, my temptation is to "force" you into agreeing with me, and to condemn you as a disloyal friend if you don't! And you end up the victim of blame and neurotic guilt just for exercising your right to independent thought. All too many a relationship both in religious life and marriage has begun to "hit the rocks" right at this point.

Tom, for example, a very sincere and devoted priest but rigid in his theology, felt that a priest should always dress in clerical attire, except on the occasions of actual participation in sports. That was a valid conclusion for himself. He felt, however, that this should be the rule for every priest and he consistently "put down" his priest friends who came to a different conclusion. John, in particular, who was also an excellent priest, felt the need to get away from the public attention which clerical clothes attract. So he chose to wear lay clothes except when he was exercising his role as a priest. That was an equally valid conclusion for John.

Not in Tom's eyes, however! He badgered John with arguments for clerical dress; openly questioned John's motives for wearing lay attire. He even threatened to end their friendship if John didn't change his way of dressing.

John got very angry at this constant pressure. Part of his anger was due to Tom's evident attempts to manipulate him. But a good part of this pain was due to the guilt feelings which were triggered off in him by Tom's constant blaming. In his mind he knew that he had the right to think for himself and to "pull his own strings," but in his feelings he felt guilty and "sneaky" as though he were trying to hide his priestly identity.

In summary, then, *any hint of blame*, explicit or implicit, actual or imagined, justified or unjustified, causes an immediate reaction in our feelings, a painful reaction of guilt or inferiority or both. Our conditioned reflex to blame makes us *feel* guilty and inferior even when there is absolutely no justification for such feelings.

It doesn't matter how the blame is given. It may be an outright accusation; it may be criticism; it may be an unrealistic expectation. It may be signals like coldness, withdrawal, looks of disdain, tones of disapproval, shouting, yelling, laughter at our words or actions, even a cold and sullen silence.

It doesn't even matter that there is no justification for the blame. I can find myself feeling guilty if I accept a cocktail and you don't. You have no intention of implying that I am slightly self-indulgent but it is easy for me to feel self-indulgent when I perceive your refusal to take a drink as blame for me because I take one. Even your continuing to work when I feel tired and decide to take a rest. You don't look at me with blame or disdain. That would be direct and actual blame and, of course, that would make me feel guilty. But just the fact that you continue to work when I have stopped working for a while, even that slight unintentional signal, can make me feel lazy, make me feel like a shirker.

All these signals are signs that my feelings interpret as blame and therefore all of them cause an immediate response of guilt or inferiority in my feelings in the same way as a pin prick causes an immediate response of pain. You blame me, and immediately I feel guilty.

Since I don't expect to feel guilty or inadequate because most often I have not done anything to merit blame, I usually don't even recognize the inappropriateness of these ugly feelings. Most often I don't even recognize what the feelings are. I don't know how to undo. I don't know how to seek reconciliation. I just feel depressed. I feel awful about myself.

When I have really done something that is morally wrong, I know how to make up for the wrong. I know how to regain peace. The devastating part about neurotic guilt is that my guilt feelings go on and on because I don't know what to do to get relief.

Roadblock to Maturity

This conditioned reflex to blame is probably the most obstructive roadblock on our path to maturity. Because of it many men continue to function as little boys; many grown women remain fixated as little girls.

Why is this so? For this reason: these vague, unlabeled feelings of guilt and inadequacy are so painful that I will do almost anything in my power to help myself from feeling them. In no way do I want to experience blame—directly or indirectly—because I *dread* the consequences of blame, the ugly depression, the feelings of guilt, the feelings of inadequacy.

Consequently, I will go to almost any lengths to avoid being blamed. I have put myself through all kinds of contortions in order to please you, or at least to keep you from being displeased with me. I know that I pay a fearful price for this protection. In at least a vague way I realize that I lose myself in the bargain. But, as long as I succeed in pleasing you, then you won't blame me or yell at me. You won't become silent or withdrawn. You won't look angry or hurt. My guilt-machine will be at rest. I won't feel those ugly consequences of blame.

When this kind of behavior becomes a pattern in my life, I become fixated at a childish level of development. I simply fail to mature. My concentration in life is not on discovering who I am, what I feel, how I would like to talk and act and live my life. My full concentration is on how I can keep myself from "ruffling your feathers," how I can avoid saying anything or doing anything that will displease you. Avoiding blame is all that matters!

Consequently, I don't think and talk and act like a mature adult. I don't act on my decisions. I don't even make any decisions! I do little more than *react* to your expectations. Everything to please you! Everything to keep you from blaming me! Like a little boy trying to please his parents! And the real "me" gets lost!

I will never make the journey to freedom until I become fully conscious of this huge roadblock in my life. I can never become truly mature, never enter my own personhood and become fully myself— until I have dismantled my guilt-machine by re-conditioning my reflex to blame.

CHAPTER VI

Dismantling My Guilt Machine:
The Path to Freedom

The purpose of the last chapter was to make myself aware of this very insidious source of psychic pain—my conditioned reflex to blame. Most of us have no idea what a devastating impact it can have on our lives. Those ugly guilt feelings which I feel immediately, whenever I am blamed, not only cause me to lose self-esteem with all the painful consequences of that loss but they can also rob me of my freedom.

Even the anticipation of blame can make me unfree. My very fear of it can turn me into a virtual coward. Because I want to avoid the blame at all costs, I do anything to appease others, make any compromise to avoid a conflict, shade any opinion, cut any corner, just to avoid being blamed.

Once I am aware of how my reflex to blame operates, that these ugly feelings plague me even when I have done absolutely nothing that is blameworthy, I have already begun my journey to freedom.

A Special Experiment

Some years ago I was anxious to bring this insight to a group of Sisters to whom I was giving a retreat. There were about thirty of them and they had been an inspiration for their attention, their silence and their manifest devotion. Toward the end of the retreat, I tried an experiment in blame. I entered the room where they were waiting for a conference and I slammed my New Testament down onto the lectern. "There's just no sense trying to give a retreat to a group like this!" I shouted with a tone of evident annoyance. "How could anybody put up with you!" I deliberately phrased my "blame" in a vague way. I had to do so. They had done nothing wrong!

I continued for a few seconds until the look of pain on their faces made me feel guilty. I couldn't go on with this charade any longer. I said, "Please forgive me. I was conducting an experiment. Would each of you kindly tell me what you were feeling those last fifteen seconds!"

The answers were a perfect revelation of the insidious and destructive effects of our reflex to blame. Each and every Sister, with very slight variations, said, "I felt awful! I felt so confused! I wondered 'What did we do!' " My blame had triggered the terrible psychic pain of guilt, a vague, neurotic guilt. Even though they had made a beautiful retreat and had done absolutely nothing to deserve blame, they felt guilty simply because I yelled at them. They not only felt the guilt and confusion but immediately they began to search to understand the reason for their pain: "What did we do?"

Not one of them asked herself: "Hey, what's the matter with him! Has he gone beserk!" That would have been the appropriate question since they had done nothing to merit my outburst. Yet not one of them asked that question. Why? Because their guilt-machine was a reflex! The stimulus of blame did not have to be reviewed and analyzed by the intellect. The stimulus of blame caused an immediate reaction of guilt.

When I explained to them what I had done, they experienced an immediate relief. Each one heaved a huge sigh of relief and evidenced a real relaxation of tension. The guilt had evaporated. They no longer felt ugly and bad, no longer confused.

I went on to explain to them that, what I had just done for them, they could learn to do for themselves in all their encounters with blame. I had identified their distress for what it was—a painful feeling of self-blame. I had also let them see how that feeling was entirely unjustified since they had done nothing wrong. They had been more "sinned against" by me than "sinning." Once they learned this process, they would be able to find wonderful peace and relief for themselves on all those occasions when they felt the biting sting of blame in any form.

Steps to Relief

For each of us, therefore, the first and foremost step in dismantling our guilt machine and *re-conditioning* our reflex to blame is to be aware of what we are feeling, whenever we are blamed. The painful discomfort is a feeling of guilt or inferiority or both. I must identify the feeling. I must name it. Acknowledge it! "I feel guilty! I feel stupid!"

Then secondly, I need to make myself aware that these feelings are inappropriate, that they don't belong to me. I need to face the truth that it is terribly unfair on my part to "buy" these ugly feelings for myself, to let myself believe them. I have to say to myself: "This is *not* my problem! I don't have to live up to this person's demands! I don't have to assume his point of view. I'll gladly give him permission to *have* his expectations but they "sure as hell" don't have to be *my* expectations!"

Just as this realization is like a cool shower on a blistering hot day, I feel a wondrous relief because now I can let the painful feelings of self-blame flow away from me like water down a drain.

When I say that these feelings are inappropriate, I am not implying that guilt feelings are never appropriate, that there can never be any real guilt! Obviously from what I have said previously, this is not the truth. Whenever I deliberately act against my conscience, willfully break the commandments of God or inflict injury on my neighbor without just cause, there I have violated justice and charity and I should feel guilty. I should feel a need to repent and to undo the wrong I have committed. My ability to recognize and to acknowledge real guilt is a sign of mature responsibility, a sign of mental and spiritual health.

The feelings we are discussing here, however, are those feelings of guilt which are triggered by blame, by unreasonable blame, which is given without any justification. Such feelings are not only neurotic but they are much more difficult for me to handle than real guilt feelings.

As strange as this may sound at first, real guilt feelings do not present a big problem for me because in real guilt I do not experience the awful confusion about my feelings. In real guilt I have done something morally wrong, so I know that what I feel is guilt! I know that what I have done is wrong. And I know what I have to do in order to make reparation and thus find relief.

Donna, for example, a Sister in her early forties, had spent her adolescence and young adulthood in heated competition with her brother for her mother's affection and attention. She won the battle but at a terrible cost. She often lied about him to her mother or grossly exaggerated his faults so that her mother would favor her more. The bitterness that resulted between them led him to ignore her. He never visited the convent on visiting days, never wrote or called. That alienation had gone on for years.

Then one day she heard from her friends that her brother was very sick. The doctors only gave him a few months to live. His approaching death made her realize with a shock all the things she had done to hurt him. She felt terribly guilty, but she knew exactly what she felt because it was real guilt. She had been cruel to him. And she knew exactly what she had to do in order to find relief. She visited him, told him how sorry she was for the way she had hurt him, and she cared for him until he died. He was touched by her kindness and forgave her—and she was able to forgive herself.

It is much different with neurotic guilt. When I feel guilty without having done anything morally wrong, I experience the depression of guilt together with a mystifying confusion about what all the pain means. And I search my mind and my heart for some explanation.

A Helpful Guideline

This confusion is distressing but it can be a very helpful guideline for me in helping me to name my neurotic guilt feelings. I can be almost sure that whenever I feel this strange and vague confusion about my painful feelings together with a strong urge to search out the reason for my discomfort, my feelings are really feelings of guilt and inadequacy, neurotic feelings, unfair and unjustified feelings. This guideline can be very helpful to me to begin the process of reconditioning my reflex to blame. I can take the first step. I can name my feelings.

Then I can go to the second step. I can say with conviction "These feelings are unfair! I have not done anything evil! I have no right to be blaming myself or looking down on myself!" Usually this brings me a tremendous sense of relief. Now I know and I feel that I am not a bad person; I've been the victim, not the culprit.

Once I've learned to master this process, I not only enjoy greater serenity in my life. I also effectively remove the huge road-block that interferes with my journey to maturity. I no longer shiver in dread at the very thought of blame. Blame now has lost its power over me. I feel a whole new well-spring of courage, the courage to think my own thoughts, to feel my own feelings. I experience the courage to make decisions and to act upon them, the unspeakably beautiful, fresh-air courage to live my own life, "to pull my own strings." And that freedom only serves to enhance further my self-esteem.

No Other Road to Freedom

Until I have mastered this key to peace, this realization that my painful feelings do not belong to me, my words and my actions, my whole life, will probably be the object of a crippling censorship, frightfully constrained by the fear of being blamed.

The distress of neurotic guilt is so painful that the very fear of it can make me a timorous coward; afraid to displease anyone, afraid of any criticism, no matter how unjustified it may be; afraid not to jump at everyone's beck and call, no matter how unfair his or her expectations and demands may be. I become a "pleaser" and an "appeaser," just to ward off any possible blame. And worst of all, in that process, I myself get lost. Instead of talking and acting as I feel I should, I constantly wonder how other people will feel about me and I react to their expectations! It is a terrible tyranny! But I suffer it and put up with it just to avoid any chance that I might be blamed.

I'll never forget the time that a fellow curate spoke to me with evident pain. He said, "The pastor would not let me go on a sick call. It came in just before lunch and he said to me: 'Come on, have your lunch first; then you can go on the call!' He wouldn't let me go! And when I got to the call right after lunch, the man was already dead!"

I felt badly for his pain. It was certainly the pain of real guilt. He should have gone on the call immediately, even if he had to knock the pastor down and step over his body! Going immediately was certainly his clear duty. He knew that and that's why he felt so guilty.

My point here is that what kept him back from responding immediately to the call was not a lack of willingness nor a lack of priestly responsibility. He was a good priest and would willingly have gone on the call the moment it came in. What stopped him from going was his fear of facing the pastor's disapproval.[1]

Incidents like this are not rare! They are legion. So many of us become "appeasers," live our life from the outside-in rather than living from the inside-out. We twist and turn ourselves into contortions worse than a pretzel, and all for the purpose of warding off blame and its painful consequences.

Awareness—The Beginning of Change

Awareness can change all that. Awareness can help me to become free—can free me to be my own person and to live my own life, free to be true to my principles, as Thomas More was true, even if the rest of the world criticizes me and heaps me with blame! The joy of that! The glorious freedom of it! I'm an adult—and I am free!

There is one final thing I can do in order to reinforce my awareness and thus begin to dismantle my guilt machine forever. I can use the reinforcement of behavior-modification techniques. I can give myself a "reward" every time I am able to bring to awareness that my feeling response to blame is a feeling of guilt or inferiority. The "reward" doesn't have to be something very big. It may be a cool drink, a respite from work, the gift of time to listen to some good music. It may even be simply the gift of self-praise. "Hey, good for you! You really did well to understand those feelings!"

The "reward" may be something small but some reward is important. It helps me to associate a pleasant experience with my

---

[1] This too was unrealistic because the pastor was also a good priest. He thought that it was a communion call rather than an emergency sick call. A communion call could have been delayed a short time.

insight and awareness (besides the very evident pleasure of relief from psychic pain). I am thus better able to re-condition my feelings and ultimately to remove this destructive reflex to blame. I'll be free at last!

The Special Beauty of Compassion and Reverence

One very important conclusion from this analysis of our reflex to blame is that compassion and reverence for others are virtues of absolutely exalted beauty. This guilt-machine of mine is not only operative in me. It is also very active in you. You are adversely affected by blame the same as I am. Any word, gesture or action that gives even the appearance of blame makes you feel guilty and inferior, just the same as it makes me feel that way. You feel the same awful confusion, the same discomfort, the insistent urge to search for meaning, the awful drive to punish yourself for being "bad."

How Christlike, then, are compassion and reverence! When I make myself become aware of your feelings and become sensitive to your pain; when I make every effort to treat you with reverence and compassion.

By compassion I enter your world of pain, I feel your pain as though it were my own. And I let you know that! I let you know that I understand how hard it is to feel guilty and ashamed, how awful it is to feel inferior. I let you know that I feel for you. I reassure you at the proper moment that I don't think that you are bad. Quite the contrary, I know that you are good. In no way do I think that you are stupid or inadequate.

Just that company in your world of feelings can mean so much. Just the fact that someone understands you, especially in those moments when it is hard for you to understand yourself! That someone understands and does not blame you!

CHAPTER VII

Rebuilding Self-Esteem: Free at Last!

The Possible Dream

The detailed explanations of our conditioned reflex to blame was a digression but one which was very important because that reflex is an insidious cause of psychic pain and a huge roadblock to freedom.

Now that the task has been completed, we can return to our study of the most formidable enemy of self-esteem, our defective perceptive system. We can take up the challenge to correct our distorted perceptions and thus rebuild our self-esteem.

I wish that there was some quick and magical way that this could be done, some easy path to remove our locked-in filters and see the true picture of our own beauty and goodness. But, unfortunately, apart from a miracle of grace, no such path exists. Changing locked-in filters and being able to identify and compensate for the mobile filters of transference and counter-transference is a very difficult task. Not an impossible task, true! But difficult and in most cases time consuming.

When the prophet Joel described the blessings of the coming Messianic age, he might well have been describing the process we need to go through. He said: "Your old men shall see visions and your young men shall dream dreams!" To regain a genuine self-esteem, we need to see a vision, a new vision of the world and, especially, a new vision of ourselves.

We also need to "dream dreams!" Before we can gain that

vision of faith by which we see ourselves as God sees us, as beautiful and good, we first have to believe that this new perceptive system is possible and attainable. That is the one dream that we have to dream. Otherwise we will never feel motivated to pay the high price that such growth requires.

This journey to freedom is a very difficult one. In its full dimensions it is the work of a lifetime. It was with good reason that Joel said that it would be "your old men" who would see visions! A relatively filter-free perceptive system is a final achievement, not an early one.

This is what this final chapter is all about—the dream and the vision—and the steps we need to take in order to progress from the first to the second.

The Indispensable Conditions

As we saw in Chapter IV, most of us have a vision of ourselves which is distorted. We perceive ourselves (in varying degrees) as lacking in goodness and beauty; see ourselves as inadequate and inferior. Often we feel trapped and helpless, as lacking the power to make our own decisions and live our own lives. Since our feelings infallibly follow our perceptions, we end up with very poor feelings about ourselves.

The process of gaining a new vision of ourselves is difficult for two reasons. Firstly, our distorted filters were impressed upon us by very significant people—our parents or parent substitutes (teachers, directors, etc.) or by experiences that were traumatic.

Secondly, these attitudes and ideals were given to us at an impressionable time in our lives—at a time when the "cement" of our developing personality was still soft and easily influenced. Once that "cement" hardened with those impressions upon it, it became most difficult to erase those impressions—especially the impressions (filters) which I developed about myself.

The task, therefore, of removing our locked-in filters cannot be accomplished with mere intellectual insights. A perception is not merely an idea. It is an interpretation of reality as we see that reality through our deep set of filters. The vision of faith, therefore, which will change the way I see myself, cannot simply be the logical, reasoned conclusions of the theologian—no matter how accurate or how exalted they may be! I can only achieve this relatively filter-free vision when I have *an entirely new experience of myself*, a corrective experience, which lets me see myself in a new and wholesome light.

Secondly, just as my original filters were implanted in me by significant persons, so now I have to have this new experience of myself in the context of a relationship, a warm and accepting relationship with a deeply significant person. This is not only terribly important; it is an absolute necessity. My original experience of myself came to me from the parents (or parent-substitutes) who defined me. It was their attitudes and ideals which became my filters. It was their evaluation of me that became my evaluation of myself. Therefore, it can only be through a new and corrective evaluation with an equally significant person that I can gain a new vision of myself—a corrective, warm, positive vision, filter-free and true! This new significant relationship is really the cutting edge by which the old filters are finally cut out.

Arthur, for example, a priest in his early forties, lived with chronic depression since his early teens. He felt such a low self-esteem that his defenses reacted with a powerful urge to excel. He "had" to excel at all times and in everything that he did. He was like a man who was driven just to prove to himself that he was not a "hopeless case." And whenever he failed to excel, when he simply did very well instead of excellently, the blow to his self-esteem was very painful.

In the course of counseling, I discovered the source of his awful self-image. He experienced himself in a relationship with a weak, ineffective mother and a negative punishing father. When he was only eleven years of age, he made a mistake and his dad screamed at him: "You're no damn good! You never were any good—and you'll never be any good!" A horrible evaluation! Absolutely untrue! But it became Arthur's evaluation of himself. At that stage in his life, his parents were his significant people.

Today, Arthur has a very different feeling about himself. He is happily married, is a trained social worker with great empathy and compassion for his clients; and he's the loving father of four children. How did that change come about? In his three years in counseling, Arthur had an entirely new and different experience of himself and of his talents in the warm and accepting relationship with his counselor.

His counselor felt very deeply for him. How could a counselor not feel that way! Arthur was a spunky man who refused to lie down and die in spite of the terrible experiences of his childhood. Step by step they walked together through those early painful experiences. Because of Arthur's transference feelings for his counselor, the counselor became "father." Thus the counselor's warm understanding, acceptance and admiration for him became for Arthur an entirely new and corrective experience of himself. He was now convinced that he was good and talented.

Later, (when he had regained enough self-esteem to risk reaching out to love) this new image of himself was reinforced by the loving acceptance and admiration of the beautiful woman he eventually married. How Arthur sees himself now can be described as nothing less than a new vision!

Our faulty, distorted perceptive system can be corrected, therefore, not by new *ideas* nor by simple good will on the part of others. Our vision cannot even be changed by honest praise and affirmation. Affection and affirmation are powerful ways of showing love but they are like toy darts against steel armor for the person with low self-esteem, unless they are given by a deeply significant person and given with a delicate sense of timing.

When I have a poor self-image, all marks of affection and affirmation are under suspicion. I simply cannot accept them in most circumstances. All compliments and praise are ineffective. I cannot believe them! You may be very sincere in giving them—and I want you to know that I appreciate your efforts to make me feel good. But the only thing that this proves to me is that *you* are good for trying to help me. It doesn't prove to me that *I* am good! I have such rotten feelings about myself, how could the nice things you are saying possibly be true!

My damaged self-esteem is the product of a damaging experience of myself in a relationship with significant persons. That image of self can be reversed only through a new and corrective experience of myself with an equally significant person. Apart from a miracle of God's grace, I know of no other path to regain self-esteem.

The Working-Through Process

Granted that these two conditions are indispensable for the journey to self-esteem and freedom, how can I begin this process? Where can I find a person whom I will allow myself to trust? A person who will have the expertise to understand me and to help me? A person who will *care* for me that much that he will go through this process with me?

Such an experience can happen in a real friendship, although, when I feel so poorly about myself, it is difficult for me to form a close friendship. It can also happen in a moving religious experience, in a relationship with Jesus. I will discuss both of these briefly later on.

The process that I would like to describe in detail is the one which is most familiar to me, and that is the corrective experience which takes place in psychoanalytic counseling and psychotherapy. I am convinced of the efficacy of this process for two reasons: one is my own personal experience in undergoing psychotherapy: the second is the constant, repeated experience of seeing hundreds and hundreds of priests and religious grow beautifully through their counseling experience at our Center.

I went for three years of personal psychoanalysis in order to experience the process from the inside, so to speak, and therefore to be a better counselor. I thought that it would be very much like attending another course at college. What a surprise I was in for! I found out that I had more "hang ups" than I could shake a stick at, neurotic processes from my own built-in filters. I could have readily spotted these in others but my defenses had completely blocked them out from my own vision. Those three years were so enlightening for me and so helpful that I have asked every counselor who works at our Center to go for at least three years for his or her own personal therapy.

I would like to describe first this process of *psychoanalytic counseling*. By studying it, we will not only see the necessary conditions for the process to be effective (given above) but also the three big stages of growth within that process, stages of a journey which I believe each person with a damaged self-esteem has to go through (more or less completely) in order to achieve a new experience of himself.

The first stage is the journey through my past in which I

experience again the pain of childhood and understand how my false perceptions were formed. The second stage is the bridge from my past to my present, the stage in which I learn to forgive. And the third stage is the one in which I learn at last to let go of my past and live in my present with my new vision.

1. The Journey Through My Past
Understanding and Compassion

It was here in my past life—and especially in my early childhood, that I formed my perceptions of other people and of myself. I wasn't born with my attitudes or prejudices. I didn't think out my ideals for myself or invent my set of values. I learned all these things through my interaction with my parents.

Agatha, a bright attractive Sister in her mid-forties, is a good example. She came for counseling because she never had a friend with whom she felt that she "came first." Her pain became more poignant and much more conscious because she thought that she had finally achieved such a friendship with a priest. However, he was apparently fearful of closeness and pulled back from her every time she used words to express her love for him. Her depression when she began counseling was excruciating. Our staff psychiatrist gave her some anti-depressants, but the relief which the medication gave was not a permanent solution for her deep depression. She needed to get at the root causes.

Agatha's early history revealed that both parents were alcoholics. She recalled incident after incident in which she literally shook with anxiety, not knowing how they would talk to her or how they would react. She recalled many examples of hurtful, rejecting things that they said to her, times of terrible fights with each other, after which one or the other would leave the home for a period of time.

As Agatha recalled and re-felt all these painful experiences, she was able to understand on a feeling level the filter of an excruciating separation-anxiety which colored her view of people. She lived with separation anxiety, never knowing when her parents would not be there for her, always fearful that she would be abandoned, and feeling, as most children do, that somehow it was her fault, that there must have been something wrong with her. She never seemed to feel the security and comfort of a qualitative parental love.

After months of staying with this pain, she was able to understand that her separation-anxiety was still very much a part of her
perceptive system in her present life; that it still influenced her
feelings and her reactions in every one of her relationships. She
desired love desperately, but she *feared* love almost as strongly. So
she was always cautious, always "held back," timid, afraid. And
her fear was contagious. While many people admired her, most
people were cautious with her because they sensed *her* caution.
They came only "so close" and no closer.

Agatha was able to realize also that her priest friend's pulling
back was not only painful in itself but it had brought back much of
the scalding pain from her childhood experiences of rejection. She
was feeling the whole childhood pain again! So she was not able to
say to herself: "I'm okay! I'm a healthy, loving woman. It's just that
my friend is fearful!" She felt that *she* was lacking and she felt
abandoned because of her own "limitations."

For me to change my distorted perceptions, I have to go
through this stage also. I have to take this journey through my past.
I need to re-experience those early learning experiences which
shaped my perceptions and set up my filters. Like Agatha, I need to
re-feel the feelings, the anxiety, the fear, the longing to please, the
steps I took to ward off the blame from my parents, the attitudes I
assumed, the unrealistic ideals that I embraced.

I need not simply an intellectual acknowledgement of what
happened, not merely an airplane trip over my past, where I review
it quickly and from a distance, so to speak. I need to walk through
it. Occasionally I need to sit down and allow myself to feel it all
again—to *cry* and to let my tears wash away some of the bitter salt
in all those old wounds.

And I need to do this in the company of someone very special
who walks through this experience with me. One who listens and
understands; one who feels the hurt with me; one who can say to
me by his manner and his tone of voice: "Wow, that was painful!
It's no wonder you felt the way you did!" That touches me. Someone understands! Someone very special. Someone with power—a
new father, a new mother. I'm not bad because I've had these
feelings! I'm not stupid! I'm human, that's all!

And then, after I have re-experienced enough of my past to
understand the *roots* of my fears, then my special person can help

me to see that this past separation-anxiety no longer has to have power over me. I'm no longer a child, who has no choice for love except his parents. I have many choices for love! I no longer lack the ability to form deep relationships. I have the tools for communication and the power to use them.

Gradually, I no longer feel like a helpless victim; no longer see myself as a prisoner of my past. The old crippling filters are beginning to come loose. I'm beginning to have a whole new experience of myself.

2. The Bridge from My Past to My Present
Forgiveness

I have to stay with my past long enough to *re-feel* all my feelings in their full dimensions, to allow myself time enough to understand how all my warped perceptions got started and why they made such a deep impression upon me. I need to see just how far they are twisted from the reality.

Then, when I have sufficiently sat in the ashes, cried the tears and understood on a feeling level that I am not the prisoner of my past, that I now have talents for interpersonal relationships that I did not have as a child, then I can begin to take the "bridge over the troubled waters" from my past to my present—the bridge of genuine emotional forgiveness.

Take Jennifer, for example, a Sister in her early fifties. It's a wonder that she ever came for counseling at all because she had so thoroughly insulated herself from all feelings, that neither pain nor joy could seem to touch her. Fortunately she was touched by the pain of loss at the death of a Sister who was the closest thing to a friend that Jennifer would allow. This loss and the empty feelings which followed from it finally penetrated her insulation enough for her to seek relief in counseling.

Her progress was extremely slow at first. Even though she was a very bright woman, highly trained professionally and in charge of a sizable agency, on the feeling level she was still like a child. She constantly laughed inappropriately; spoke in a high shrill voice. She denied that there was any pain for her from the conflicts at her job or from the put-downs at her convent, put-downs that would have torn the ordinary person to shreds. Even her pain of loss at her "friend's" death was not felt as deeply as it should have been—especially since there was not another person who was meaningful in her life. All of her feelings were either completely denied or minimized to the point of being meaningless.

Working with her was painful for me. I was hurting for some of the conflicts she was facing and she acted as though they were just "water off a duck's back." Gradually, however, I was able to encourage her to talk about her early childhood and young girlhood. And then, fortunately, she began to feel; tight lips at first to choke back emotion, periods of silence in which she swallowed the pain that was longing to come out, and finally tears, tears in torrents and sobs that shook her whole body.

She revealed how her mother was mentally sick. She had been hospitalized on several occasions. Her dad was ineffectual. He denied that there was anything wrong with her mother. Those times when her mother was home from the hospital she treated Jennifer and her brother like toy dolls. They were dressed immaculately but never allowed to move off the chair where she sat them; never allowed to speak unless spoken to; never allowed to accept cookies or candy (they might get dirty!) from anyone. Their answer had to be "No, thank you!" Most hurtful of all, they were never allowed to cry or talk above a whisper or express any feelings.

Disobedience of these directives brought with it swift and severe punishment. Jennifer's only outlet was her studies. There she performed brilliantly. Her mind grew to be sharp and sophisticated. But emotionally, her filters were so distorted that she felt guilty and ashamed about having *any feelings.* Consequently she had surrounded herself with insulation. In effect, she had become emotionally numb.

After she passed through the first stage of her counseling, understanding on a feeling level all that had happened to her, Jennifer had to cross the bridge from her past to her present. That bridge had to be the passageway of true emotional forgiveness.

This was difficult for her. Indeed it is difficult for most of us, because there is such a vast difference between forgiveness as an act of the will and forgiveness as an emotional experience.

Forgiveness as an act of the will is an openness of mind to forgiveness. It may even be a desire on my part to forgive you when you have hurt me. But I *cannot force my feelings* to feel close to you again. As long as the hurt is still there, the arrow of your unkindness still imbedded in my feelings, all I can feel is pain and the "need" to be far away from you. I can have forgiveness as an act of the will (the decision to forgive, which Jesus called for when He urged us to forgive "not seven times but seventy times seven times"). That is, I can command myself to want to forgive you. However, I cannot command emotional forgiveness. I cannot command my feelings to feel close to you again!

Emotional forgiveness is something much more beautiful and healing. In emotional forgiveness I not only want to forgive you; I do forgive you. I feel close to you again. The arrow has been removed; the wound has been healed; the pain is gone.

In order for me to experience emotional forgiveness, two conditions are necessary. First, I have to hear you acknowledge my pain. I have to realize that you know that you have hurt me. I have to hear you say that.

Even if the hurt felt was due to a misunderstanding on my part, and therefore not your fault at all, I still have to hear you *acknowledge* that I was hurt. Or even if the hurt was for my own good, a helpful criticism, a necessary rebuke, even here I have to hear you say that you realize that I was hurt, that you wish there could have been an easier way. I have to hear you say this or else I cannot feel close to you again.

Secondly, I have to hear you say that you are sorry; that you *regret* the unkind words, the hurtful gesture, the sarcastic remark. I have to hear you say that you wish you could live that moment over again, because then you would not hurt me. You regret the fact that I was hurt.

Once I hear you say both these things sincerely and with feeling, wow! almost immediately I feel very close to you again. I don't have to command my feelings to feel warmly about you again; they simply do! The experience of emotional forgiveness is one of the most beautiful experiences in life. It brings us back to emotional intimacy. It's like coming home to a blazing fireplace after being out in the cold.

Jennifer had to go through this second stage of her therapy if she was going to pass over the bridge from her past to her present. But how could she get her mother, who was still a mentally sick woman, to acknowledge her pain and express adequate sorrow for that pain? Her mother was incapable of such insight and feeling. The only way that Jennifer was able to achieve emotional forgiveness was in her relationship with her counselor, her substitute parent, who could now speak in her mother's place.

This is where the phenomenon of transference can be a great help in the counseling process. Unconsciously Jennifer's mobile filter of transference was triggered into place through the counseling process and she saw and felt about me as she felt about her mother. So, when she spoke with great pain about the many hurtful things her mother did, I was able to acknowledge her pain, able to feel the hurt with her and understand how desperately lonely and misunderstood she felt. And because I was now "mother," a mother-substitute, to Jennifer's feelings, it was like her mother herself acknowledging her pain.

I was also able to express regret for what her mother did. It was unfair and unjust that a good and innocent child should have been treated so poorly. I was awfully sorry that mother had been so cruel! That meant a great deal to Jennifer. There was visible relief in the muscles of her face. The conditions for emotional forgiveness had been fulfilled. And while she still was not able to feel close to her mother again, it was beautiful to see how she was now able to understand emotionally that her mother was sick, that there was no intentional malice in the things her mother had done. It was easy now for her to feel forgiveness for her mother.

She also came to the point where she was able to feel forgiveness for herself. It was not Jennifer's fault that her mother was cruel. All the blame and unrealistic expectations that came from her mother (which had caused Jennifer to feel so much anger for her mother!)— Jennifer no longer felt guilty for that anger. Her mother's sickness was unfortunate, but it was nobody's fault—certainly not Jennifer's! Emotionally, she had now "forgiven" herself!

3. Living in My Present
The New Vision

Now that Jennifer had experienced emotional forgiveness, she was ready at last to let go, to give up the past pain and to change the filters which this pain had caused.

The experience of allowing herself to feel all her feelings, even the painful ones, was very freeing for her. The ability to sob and cry, to cry freely and without shame, was a genuine therapeutic release. She could appreciate the change in herself; the rigid muscles now relaxed, the tense facial expressions now at ease, her coldness and aloofness now giving way to availability and warmth. She had had a new experience of herself, an experience that she felt comfortable with, a picture of herself that she liked very much.

It was relatively easy now for her to let go of the built-in filter that feelings are ugly and bad. She had experienced just the opposite. She was no longer the little girl that couldn't get messy, or express any feeling or even cry. Now she knew what feelings are really like—that they are like the colors of the rainbow. She realized now that feelings add beauty and power to life. She no longer felt guilty for having feelings, no longer felt ugly and inadequate, even for her negative feelings. Feeling jealous wasn't the same as hurting another. Her feelings just showed that she was very much alive!

Jennifer never quite got to that point where feelings made her feel beautiful. Some little part of her old filter remained; some little perceptions that "feelings were good, but . . . !" Her feelings, however, no longer caused psychic pain. She was able to accept them as an integral part of her personality and live with them in peace. At least to that extent she had let go.

In my own journey this is the last step for me also. Once I have experienced emotional forgiveness for myself and for the significant people who have hurt me in my past life, I also am ready at last to let go. I can let go of my past pain. And I can let go of the filters which that past pain had erected, the filters which were still exercising a powerful influence on my perceptions and my feelings and my life.

I understand the false programming now. I've seen for myself just how my distortions were formed. I have worked through the scalding bitterness and the pain. I'm now able to appreciate what my parents had to face; to understand all the "hang ups" which they inherited from their parents. They too were victims. I can appreciate that now!

I can also appreciate that many of my parents' words and actions, which I took as rejection, were really not signs of rejection at all but only their way of dealing with their own pain. It's more clear to me now that the hurts, which I felt, were not really proofs that they did not love me. Almost always I find that they did love me! In their own way and with their own limitations, they did love me. They were simply inadequate in knowing how to make that clear to me. Emotional forgiveness at last is easy for me, forgiveness for them, forgiveness for myself.

I have finally come over the crest of the hill. No more uphill struggle! I can let go now and descend leisurely into the green valley of my true self, let go of all the bitterness, all the suffocating feelings of helplessness, all the distortions and unrealistic ideals. I can descend into the luscious green valley of my own humanness and dwell there in peace—no longer ashamed of my shadow side, convinced at last that my combination of lights and shadows make me much more attractive and genuine than all my pretenses at lily-white perfectionism!

With St. Paul I can say, "Therefore, I will glory in my infirmities that the strengths of Christ may be manifest in me . . . for when I am weak, then I am strong." The "all-or-nothing" filter which caused me endless trouble in the past has now crumbled beneath this new experience of the me that is imperfect—*imperfectly okay*! Nor do I have to defeat you in a discussion in order to feel good about myself. We can listen to each other and respect each other's point of view—even if we have widely different views. Our conversations are not on a win-or-lose basis! We share in order to understand each other, not to conquer each other. I'm no longer out to win an argument! I'm out to win a person!

Francis, for example, was just ordained a few years when he was overcome by depression. It didn't seem to be a reactive depression due to any recent loss or disappointment but more of a chronic depression which became more acute as he felt more and more inadequate in his priestly work.

Francis' past history revealed that he felt his dad constantly compared him with his brother, John. Subsequent sessions helped clarify that the comparisons were more on Francis' part than on the part of his dad—but Francis could not see that until much later in his counseling.

John apparently had a scintillating personality. He was a great athlete, a brilliant student, and he was very popular with the young people of the neighborhood. Francis felt "like a clod!" next to John. He was very shy and quiet, just above average in sports and a little bit less than average in his studies.

It seemed to Francis that his "dad's eyes lit up" whenever John was around. He went to all the games in which John played and seemed so proud of John's achievements. On several occasions when John was the "life of the party," his dad said to Francis, "Why are you so quiet? Why don't you speak up?" Francis heard this not as his dad reaching out to him but as criticism, as his dad's inability to accept Francis for himself.

As a result of this unresolved sibling rivalry, in which he came out as the "loser," Francis grew up with strong inferiority feelings. He had taken on his dad's "evaluation" of him as his own. He couldn't stand his own quietness and shyness. He felt so guilty about his jealousy for John, that he denied it completely, and even took John's name as his own religious name in his community. Tied in with his jealousy and anger for John was a very genuine love and admiration for John. He just seemed overwhelmed with a mass of confusing feelings.

He felt that his work as chaplain at a huge hospital demanded a personality that was outgoing and friendly—a personality like John's, certainly not a quiet, retiring personality like his own! Each day he felt more inadequate and more depressed.

The counseling process was difficult at first. Even though he was in great pain, he was extremely quiet. Even the most gentle and open-ended questioning on my part was seen by him as just one more case of parental pressure for him to "talk up." Since I was now "father" through the transference, he saw my interest as a rejection of his personality and a "demand" that he be more like John.

I had to be very patient and allow him to move very slowly. Only one thing did I insist on—I would not call him by his religious name of John; I always called him Francis, hoping he would understand that I didn't want him to be anyone other than himself.

Gradually all the pain came out. He went through the first stage. He re-felt the pain of his dad's "rejection" and his own rejection of himself. He was able to talk about his sibling rivalry—at first with unbelievable shame and guilt. I let him stay with it, sit with it, feel it all over again. And then gradually I was able to move him toward forgiveness: "You loved your dad! How could you not be tempted to become John instead of being Francis!"

It wasn't only my "fatherly" acceptance of him as Francis that helped him. I invited him to be part of a group and they probably did more than I did in bringing him to acceptance and forgiveness. They were comfortable with his silence and shyness. And when he did speak, they were very appreciative of his insights, which in truth were very profound. One Sister in particular gave him a new vision of himself. She learned to love him dearly and let him know it in a gradual, non-threatening way.

Then Francis was ready, ready to let go of his old perceptions of himself, his old unrealistic demands that he had to be John in order to be acceptable. He was able to descend into the valley that was Francis—with his lights and shadows—and dwell there at last with genuine serenity and peace.

At this point in his life his relationship with his dad is very warm. To his surprise, his dad seeks for his advice and opinions and admires him for himself. He has a new sense of self-esteem and confidence. The once shy and bashful man is filled with self-confidence.

The New Vision

The final result of this working-through process is a new vision—a new vision of people, a new understanding and acceptance of them, and, more wonderful still, a new vision of myself.

I begin to see that the objective and unadulterated truth is that every human being is basically beautiful and *good*. It's true that all of us have been wounded by original sin. And we have been further damaged by hurtful experiences in our childhood. It's true also that we ourselves have added to that damage by our own mismanagement of our feelings—by our sinfulness. We can act in mean and hateful ways. We can give in to moods, become terribly defensive. We can lock others out of our world. That's all true. We are wounded.

But get behind the barbed wire of our defenses, rip away the mask of our hateful behavior, and inside we'll find a scared and timid person who just hungers to be understood and to be loved. No matter how hateful we may act! No matter how we may seem to fight against love! Rip away the mask and down deep we are hoping against hope that people will see us for what we really are and love us for ourselves. We want to love and we want to be loved. That's the truth of the matter and that makes us beautiful, even when we cannot see it or appreciate it for ourselves. Once we see this vision of people's basic beauty, it is much easier for us to reach out to them and love them.

Also, each one of us is *adequate* for the special role that God has planned for us to fulfill. We are different—just as parts of the body are different because each part is made for a special task. Our only problem comes when we don't have reverence for our differences and for our uniqueness. Then, instead of loving ourselves as we are, we end up in the frustrating fantasy world of craving to be somebody else! Then we feel inadequate because we don't have the other person's talents.

The new vision lets us see that we don't have to make the talents of others! We don't need them!

An ear isn't equipped to think. That doesn't make it an inferior ear! An ear is inferior only if it is so depressed about not thinking that it forgets to listen and to hear! We are never inadequate at being ourselves! We are only inadequate at trying to be someone else!

When I am fixing a little gadget and I need the exact size to hold it all together, nothing but that precise nut will do the job. And when I find it, I'm absolutely thrilled with it—as though I have found a pearl!

The new vision of faith lets me see that the same truth applies to people. People come in all sizes and shapes, with a whole different array of talents and personalities. But each one is specially designed by God for a unique work in life. And for that special work each one is *more than adequate*, even if at times he may seem like a little "nut!"

And finally, each one of us has *power*, power to live our own life and make our own decisions. This does not mean power over others! Power over others is not true or healthy power, not for them, not for ourselves. True power, that life-giving power which really enhances our self-esteem, is power over ourselves.

We human beings need to feel that we have this inner power. Few things are more aggravating and frustrating for us than the feeling of helplessness—that choking feeling that we are victims, either pushed around by some blind forces of fate or manipulated by powerful institutions or powerful persons.

An interesting study conducted recently with white rats revealed how this feeling of helplessness can be devastating, even to the lower animals. Two groups of rats were put in separate cages. Both cages were wired so that the rats could be given painful electric shocks by the psychologist conducting the experiment. The only difference between the cages was that the first cage had a small wheel which the rats could turn in order to shut off the electric current. They soon learned this and, whenever a shock was administered, one of the rats in the first cage would immediately run to the control wheel and turn off the electricity.

The cages were so wired that the electricity would also be turned off in the second cage at the very same moment it was turned off in the first cage. The only difference was the difference in control. The first group was not helpless. They could relieve their pain. The second group suffered no more electric shock than the first group but they had no control in shutting off the current.

After a few months both groups were killed and their bodies examined for physical symptoms of stress. The rats of the second group were in much worse shape than those of the first group. They had enlarged hearts from their very high blood pressure, ulcers, diverticulitis, arthritis, etc. Apparently, it was not the stress of the electric shock that caused their greatest pain. It was their feeling of helplessness; their lack of control.

The degree of the pain of helplessness is even greater in human beings. Some fascinating studies done in recent years with victims (New York Times, January 17, 1984) revealed, contrary to the popular opinion, "that people, who blame themselves, at least in part, for becoming the victim of a crime or an accident or an illness, have less difficulty coping with the event" than those who feel that they were in no way to blame. This was true of women who had been raped, or wives who had been battered, as well as accident victims and persons suffering from cancer.

When we realize how terribly painful feelings of guilt are, we naturally wonder why these victims would embrace guilt. How could such painful feelings serve in any way as a relief for their over-all pain?

The researchers concluded that the apparent reason was that even the pain of guilt was more acceptable and easier to bear than the feeling of helplessness. They felt that, if in some way they were responsible for being victimized, then they had it within their power not to let that happen again. That feeling of responsibility gave them a sense of control; a sense that they could so something about avoiding such disasters in the future. Apparently that sense of control made them feel so much more secure that it was worth feeling guilty in order to have that control!

The new vision helps me to see that all human beings are endowed by God with this basic power and control over their own lives. There is no need for any of us to feel like victims.

We are not in the hands of any blind force of fate. Nor need we be the helpless victims of the manipulations of others. The truth is that we are in the House of a loving Father Who won't let anything happen to us that isn't ultimately for our own good. That's how He treats even the birds of the air. "Are we not of much greater value than they?" (Matt. 5, 26) Nor are we helpless before others. We may not be able to change them or prevent them from being manipulative and unjust. But we have the power to decide how we will *respond* to their injustice. We can assert ourselves in the hope that they will then respect our rights. And we can pull back from them completely if even assertion fails. We can seek out people with whom we can relate warmly and situations in life which are truly fulfilling. And all this without guilt! The new vision lets us see that we not only have the power to pull our own strings; we also have the *right* to do so. We are not bad when we assume control of our life. On the contrary, we are mature and good—*and free*!

A clear example of this basic ability was Mary, a woman in her late thirties who had desired for years to enter religious life but felt blocked from her goal by guilt and the manipulation of her brothers. Her dad had died when she was in her early twenties and her brothers insisted that the entire care of their mother rested upon her shoulders. That care was particularly difficult because her mother was so dependent, that she wouldn't let Mary out of her sight.

Mary felt absolutely trapped. It was a "Catch-22." If she fulfilled her dream by entering the monastery, she would have felt terribly guilty for "abandoning" her mother. When she continued to devote all her time to her mother, she felt helpless and trapped— and extremely angry at both her mother and her brothers. There seemed to be no way out!

Occasionally she would break away from her mother for a few hours of "breathing" time with her friends. However, she paid dearly for those moments of freedom because both her mother and her brothers would heap abuse upon her and make her feel guilty and unworthy. Then, for a time, she would deny herself the opportunity to go out with her friends only to feel smothered and helpless once more. In either case, her self-esteem suffered painful blows.

In the course of counseling and with some excellent support from the members of her group at the center, she developed a new understanding of how manipulative her family had been with her. She came also to a new perception of her own worth and dignity; she began to sense both her right and her power to make her own decisions and to lead her own life. She entered the monastery, her chosen life-style, just as her brothers had chosen their life-style all these years. Her brothers finally had to assume their share of the responsibility of caring for their mother. Mary described her working-through process as "coming into God's free air and sunshine for the first time in my life!"

This new vision makes it easier for me to understand our human nature, to accept people where they are on their journey; easier for me to respect them and to love them. It also helps me to know how to help them to come to a greater appreciation of themselves.

New Vision of Myself

Probably the most rewarding effect of the counseling process is the new vision I now have about myself. It is this new vision which brings me the ultimate relief from psychic pain and the untold joy of a vibrant self-esteem.

As I go through the three stages, I can truly achieve a whole new experience of myself—a positive, corrective experience in relationship with my new significant person. Each one of my locked-in filters comes up for review before my new "authority" person and before my own new, keener vision.

I can let myself feel the pain that the distorted filters have caused me. I can cry without shame. I can let my special person show me compassion. I can even feel a deep compassion for myself. I can forgive myself! And then, I can let go, let go of all the false filters and unrealistic standards, and enjoy the real beauty and goodness of myself, a goodness that was there all the time but hidden from my perception.

Some years ago, I was privileged to meet a young black girl at a Cursillo center who was a living example of how a true standard of beauty could enlighten a person's life. The priests at the Center had asked me to experience a weekend cursillo in order to evaluate the psychological soundness of the cursillo experience. (It was, of course, thoroughly sound and inspiring!)

Helen, the young black girl, was one of the "angels," i.e., one of the teenagers who volunteered to wait on tables. She was a puzzle to me at first. I very seldom think that a person is homely but I did feel that she was. Her features were distorted quite severely, and yet, in her personality, she was positively beautiful. She was cheerful, kind, bubbly, and very generous. She just seemed to radiate self-esteem. I couldn't figure her out until that Sunday afternoon when her parents came to pick her up. Oh Lord! It was so inspiring to see their greeting! They hugged her and kissed her. They told her how proud they were of her that she had served on that weekend. Her dad lifted her off the ground with his hug and swung her around. She beamed with joy. It was very moving!

Then I knew her secret! *They* were the significant people in her life and therefore their perception of her simply blotted out any other perception, including the Hollywood standard of beauty, the general prejudice against black people that she surely experienced, even the cruelty of other children's remarks about her facial features. All these were simply blotted out. She was beautiful to her parents, so she was beautiful in her own eyes. And she lived and spoke and acted beautifully. She was an absolute delight!

Genuine counseling can re-create that same kind of an experience for me even though I have had a negative view of myself up to now. The skillful counselor allows my transference to reach the appropriate depth, the depth which is most helpful to me. He will let me experience negative transference with all its unrealistic expectations and demands, only as long as I need to feel those feelings from my past, cry for them, understand the distortions, and then finally let them go. During this process he interprets for me what I have been feeling—until my anger for him is gone, and my anger for my parents as well.

Then the skillful counselor capitalizes on the positive transference to heal my open sores. Because I make him "all-knowing, all-

wise, all-good," I endow him with the same authority and "infalli-
bility" with which I endowed my parents as a child. Once he
"possesses" these qualities in my eyes then he can help me first to
question my distorted filters and then to *let them go*. His "infallible
wisdom" is the cutting edge by which I can sever their hold on me
and discard them. He can say to me, "Oh, so you were not
absolutely perfect! Mmmm! Does that mean that you're a complete washout? How in God's name do you draw that conclusion!
That does not follow. I have done a great many things in my life
that are right and good. Let me relish that, rather than blame
myself for what I failed to do!"

I also find myself thinking, "He obviously enjoys me as a
person, my sense of humor, my honest struggles to be real. Lord,
that approval feels good!" Gradually I find myself beginning to
appreciate and enjoy myself. What has happened? I've had a whole
new and corrective experience of myself—and *now I like what I see*!
What Helen's parents did for her from early childhood, my counselor and the counseling experience has now done for me.

I remember a similar experience from my own childhood.
There were nine children in our family and I was the oldest of the
bottom five who were still in grammar school. My mother had a
custom of giving us a quarter when we got promoted. One particular year at promotion time, we all ran home as usual to collect our
quarters, myself, Pat, who is now a Josephite Sister, Dan, Gerri,
and Joan. All of us were delighted except Gerri. We didn't realize it
then but Gerri was losing her hearing, so she had failed and was left
back. I presented my report card and got my quarter. Pat and Dan
did the same. Then Gerri came with tears in her eyes. I'll never
forget what my mother did when Gerri gave her the report card.
She said, "Gerri, here's fifty cents for getting left back!"

Even though I was just a kid, I was touched by that lovely
gesture. Gerri's pain was great enough! My mother just seemed to
know instinctively that Gerri's self-esteem had been wounded and
needed healing. Gerri herself was really cute. She looked at my
mother through her tears and said: "Mom, don't you know that
getting left back is bad?" My mother just hugged her and answered:
"Gerri, *you're* not bad. You're good!" It was just the right thing!

What a proper sense of values my mother was teaching us, that human feelings are of much greater value than good marks or success.

New Sense of Power and Adequacy

It isn't only the new experience of myself as good that I can gain from counseling. I also gain an experience of myself as adequate and as powerful.

Marguerite, for example, a Sister in her early forties, had always considered herself inadequate because she was lacking in verbal skills. She had barely managed to get her bachelor's degree after years and years of part-time study because exams terrified her. She knew the material but felt tongue-tied when asked to express it. She was especially threatened and anxiety ridden if she had to express herself in the presence of others.

During the course of her counseling, I began to appreciate what a deeply feeling woman she was and how sensitive she was of the feelings of others. Her sensitivity made her intuitive with the children she taught and truly creative in her teaching. Once she was in her own classroom without any supervisor present, she felt free to "do her thing," to use all her teaching skills. She not only taught the children the subject matter; she also gave them a sense of their own worth and beauty.

The very first thing she would do when she started with a new class was to ask them to copy a paragraph from their text book. She gave no further instructions. The results were usually disastrous. Some used crayons and scraps of paper, others pencils and pens. Most of the writing was illegible. She had each child put his/her name on the papers and then she collected them and put them in the top drawer of her desk.

Then, for a few minutes each day she taught them how to write, how to form letters neatly and space them properly. After two months, she'd ask them to take a sheet of paper and write out the same paragraph from their textbook, again with no further instruction. As they were finishing, she went around the class and gave each one of their original sample of writing. The difference between the two was so remarkable that each child was thrilled.

She then put both copies side by side in a V form and tacked them to the bulletin board with the child's picture in between the pages. When the parents came with the children for parents' night each child was able to show off his/her achievement. Marguerite had not only taught them to write well. She gave them a lovely sense of their own ability and worth!

Sam, for example, was a professional man in his early forties, a man who was very bright and successful in his field. He was insightful about the struggles of his clients. And yet, in the presence of his wife, he seemed literally to shrink into a state of passivity and fear. I could hardly believe how nervously he spoke and acted when she came with him for one session. Whenever he was with her, every word he spoke, every gesture, each tone of voice were all geared to placating her and to keep her from getting angry.

He rebelled in some ways. He dated other women, moved out of the house and got his own apartment. He also drank too much. Even these token attempts, however, at assuming power over his life were only the other side of the coin of his paralyzing fear that it was she who had all the power and all the control. Even though he had his own apartment, he "dutifully" called her every night "to report" and went home every weekend to follow her plans for the weekend. If he was busy and couldn't call until late in the evening, his hands would shake with fear. His feeling of helplessness greatly lessened his self-esteem. "I feel like a coward," he would say. "I feel like a little boy!"

Past history revealed that Sam had a very good relationship with his father who loved his sense of humor and took pride in his athletic prowess. But his mother was cold and distant and hard to please. Sam tried very hard to win her approval but never felt sure that she really loved him or accepted him for himself.

As counseling progressed, he was able to appreciate why he had chosen Evelyn to be his wife. Evelyn's personality was very similar to his mother's. She was cool and distant, unsure of herself, hard to please. Unconsciously Sam had been the victim of repetition-compulsion, a compulsion to solve in his adult life a problem he failed to solve in his childhood. He had never felt that he had been fully accepted by his mother. Consequently, the hunger he felt for mother's acceptance never died in him. When he looked for a wife, unconsciously he sought for a woman who was just like his mother in the hope that this time he could make it with "mother." This time he could finally win her full acceptance.

After some time in counseling Sam was able to make this insight his own. It helped him to understand his terror in Evelyn's presence. Then gradually he was able to take the risk of asserting himself with Evelyn. He returned home, but not as a little boy trying to placate Evelyn, but as a man trying to be himself and work out his relationship with her on a peer level, a healthy man-woman level. His "acting-out" rebellions of dating other women and drinking too much all stopped. Because he felt more secure now about his *right* to be himself and his power to assert himself, he didn't have to prove anything. He had a new experience of himself as a man.

Counseling and psychotherapy are safe and sure ways to deal with the agony of psychic pain, sure ways to regain self-esteem. The only difference between the two is that in psychotherapy the therapist allows the transference relation to deepen into a transference neurosis for those clients whose defenses are more intransient. That is, he is less active in the process, especially in the beginning, thus encouraging a stronger and deeper transference, one in which the client feels the childhood pains and distortions more acutely until his denial and repression of them is no longer possible.

Apart from that difference, both counselor and psychotherapist use the same approach, the same "tools" of warm, positive regard, purposeful ventilation of feelings, dealing with resistance and the working through of transference, thus giving the client what he most needs: a new, corrective experience of himself and of other people, a new vision.

Counting the Cost

The cost of such therapy, admittedly, is quite high, not only in terms of time and money but also in terms of commitment to a process that is painful.

It is understandable that both the clients themselves as well as their religious superiors and friends might question the whole process—especially in the early stages when the client (in re-experiencing his past) may seem to get worse rather than better. Doubts creep in also when a client begins the process of working-through and tries to make changes in his life. If he has been passive and unassertive, for example, it is quite possible that, in his effort to become more assertive, he may temporarily go to the opposite extreme and become aggressive and abrasive. Previously he was afraid to sign out a car. Now he signs one out "eight days a week!" Admittedly, such behavior is hard to take, and those who have to live with him, as well as his superiors, might easily place the blame on the counseling process itself. (They, of course, should confront him about such behavior! Only then will he learn the proper boundaries for his life. If their confrontation causes him pain, he can deal with that pain with his counselor who will help him face the reality of social boundaries.)

It is very helpful when both religious themselves, as well as their superiors, understand that the merits of counseling cannot be judged on the basis of quick results. It's a long process and it can only be fairly measured by its final outcome. And once a client is truly motivated and works through his pain with an adequately trained counselor, the process usually does work. And it ends in a new birth, a resurrection and a new psychic life.

Other Paths to Self-Esteem

There are other ways to regain a lost self-esteem besides the path of counseling. They can be outlined more briefly because the basic conditions for them to be effective are the same as the basic conditions for counseling. The three stages of growth through which a person must pass are also essentially the same. These have already been treated in detail.

There are four other paths to self-esteem besides counseling and psychotherapy:

1. The experience of qualitative love from a parent substitute;

2. The experience of spiritual conversion through a deep relationship with Jesus;

3. The experience of growth through insightful spiritual direction;

4. The experience of love in a deep friendship with a peer.

1. Love from a Parent-Substitute

A person who has been emotionally deprived in childhood because his parents were not sufficiently present to his need (either due to death or alcoholism or to the parents' own neurotic struggles), such a person can have his needs met adequately by a loving parent-substitute.

Very often this happens through the legal process of adoption. A happily married couple, who cannot have children of their own, often make ideal parents to an orphan child.

Brigid, a delightful young woman of twenty-three, is a good example. Even though she was twenty-seven months old when she was adopted, she was very over-weight and emotionally deprived. Her parents were killed when she was just an infant and she had been in several foster homes where she was mistreated, just given "junk food" to keep her from crying.

Her adopting parents were very loving people. They were patient with her crying and her fears. They spent time with her, bought her dolls and toys and showed her a lot of affection. She grew up beautifully in every way. She lost her excess weight, did well in school, took an active part in parish activities—and became very popular with the boys and girls in her crowd. To my mind, she just exudes self-esteem. Her adopting parents gave her a truly loving experience of herself.

At times, a parent-substitute may be a Sister in school, a parish priest, a volunteer Big Brother or Big Sister. As long as the two essential elements are operative, this creative healing can take place. The parent-substitute has to care, with a care that is evident to the child in the form of positive acceptance and regard. And, secondly, the child has to get a new, corrective experience of his worth within this warm and loving acceptance.

Many years ago, a sociology professor at a large American University gave his class the assignment of interviewing one hundred teenagers from the city's ghetto. Their findings were very discouraging. Many of the teenagers were from broken families. Social and employment opportunities were very slim. When the professor asked his students to evaluate the chances that these teenagers had for success in life, their general estimate was that it was quite low.

The reports were all put away until approximately twenty-five years later when they were discovered by the head of the sociology department. He conceived an interesting idea. He asked his class to try to find the men and women from the original study in order to see how they had made out in life. Fortunately, the students were able to find seventy-six of the original one hundred. To their surprise, almost all of the subjects were successfully employed and fairly well-adjusted in their personal lives. Some were professional people; some business people; most were either employed and/or happily married.

The head of the department couldn't understand these findings. He read carefully through all the reports in an effort to discover some clue which would explain the unexpected success of the subjects of the study. Finally, he found a clue. Almost all of them mentioned with great reverence one of their high school teachers. The professor thought to himself: "I wonder if she's still living. I'd love to meet her and explore her methods."

He contacted the Board of Education and found out that she was retired but still alive and alert. He contacted her, told her about the study project and made an appointment to meet with her. He showed her all the case histories. She would smile with recognition and say, "Oh Tommy, of course, I remember him. He was slow, but he worked so hard."

The professor was overcome with admiration. He said to her: "Do you realize that you are the single most significant factor that accounts for their success and their emotional adjustment! What is your magic?" She smiled and replied: "Gee, I don't have any magic! I just know that I really loved them!" That was her magic. She was a loving substitute parent and what a difference her loving care meant in their lives.

2. Spiritual Conversion

The psychic pain of inferiority and self-hatred can also be relieved through a spiritual conversion. "Lord, by Your cross and resurrection, You have set us *free!*" Once I realize how much I am cherished and loved by God, I am almost bound to feel lovable and adequate. God, Who knows each one through and through, so loves me that He sent His Son to die for me. I really must be worthwhile!

St. Paul felt this very deeply and exclaimed, "He loved me—and delivered Himself up for me!" (Gal. 2, 20)

This realization of God's love in Christ meant so much to St. Paul that he chose the image of Jesus crucified as his one, all-powerful tool to convert the Corinthians. Corinth was the moral cesspool of the Roman Empire, filled with cut-throats, prostitutes, thieves. As Paul sat on the ship which was bringing him to Corinth, he wondered how he could teach such people about gentleness, humility, love for each other. And then, he began to realize that people *act* in ugly ways because they feel ugly about themselves. Their words and actions are mostly the outward expression of their own terrible self-concept. So Paul determined to help them perceive their real beauty and worth in the same way that he had discovered his—by appreciating how valuable he was in the eyes of Jesus! In writing to them later, he said: "I determined to know nothing among you except Christ, and Him crucified!" (I Cor. 2:2) He was saying in effect, "You think that you are ugly! No way! Look at the price that Jesus paid for you! You're beautiful in His eyes, so you must be beautiful in fact!"

There's no doubt that this perception of God's love, this realization that Jesus loves me as a friend, can give me a whole new experience of my worth and goodness. The problem is, as always when one is afflicted with low self-esteem, how do I make myself realize that it is myself that is loved in such a special way? Why would Jesus love me or die for me? I can understand that He died for other people, but for me? Or, if I do believe it, then I'm convinced that it is only because He is so noble and good, not because I am! I feel too worthless to let His love touch me or heal me.

Spiritual conversion is a break-through in which my mere acknowledgement of Jesus' love becomes my perception and realization of His love. Sometimes this happens through a deeply moving retreat experience. Sometimes it occurs in a spiritual rebirth in a charismatic experience. I have not had the opportunity personally to "walk" with such persons before, during, and after their conversion. I wish that I had. I have met a number of priests, however, religious and laity who have shared this experience with me, and it really changed their lives. They felt beautiful after their conversion. They felt free.

The same experience can happen to those who get to know

Jesus through daily, loving meditation on the Gospel story. The Gospel is a living word. Like Jesus himself, it is "yesterday, today and forever." (Heb. 13, 8) When I make a sincere effort to see Jesus there, to experience Him as He lived and talked and felt and spoke, it is almost impossible for me not to admire Him and love Him. I find myself wanting to be like Him, to think like Him, to share His values. Gradually I begin to believe on a feeling level that He loves me even more than I love Him. I realize, as I never did before, that He is not dead, that He is alive and present to me, that He and I have a relationship, that we are friends.

Such a realization only increases my hunger to know Him even more, as He really is, to share myself with Him as I really am, with my confusion, my pain, my awful feelings about myself. And I begin to experience His acceptance of me just as I am, right now, with all my limitations and faults. His only question to me is the question to Simon Peter: "Do you love Me?" That's all that really matters to Him. I don't have to be perfect. I'm all right as I am. I begin to think and to feel about myself with a new vision.[1]

3. Spiritual Direction

A depressed person with little self-esteem can often find a new and corrective experience of himself through the positive regard and care of an insightful spiritual director.

It is important that a spiritual director, besides having the necessary human qualities of sensitivity and concern for others, have special training in the various branches of theology and in the dynamics of the human personality. It would be ideal if he were to become a counselor first and have a few years of clinical supervision. The skills he would acquire here would be invaluable for his practice of spiritual direction. Understanding the client's relationship with God becomes much more clear when he can appreciate the client's natural drives and defenses and his relationship with himself.

Some years ago, Ruth, a Sister in her mid-thirties, was struggling to cope with a huge amount of hurt and anger. She had very

---

[1]The author's own two books of meditation may prove helpful: *Meditation on the Gospel; Meditation on St. Paul*, published by the Confraternity of the Precious Blood, Brooklyn, NY.

little impulse control. Her anger often came out in the form of sarcastic remarks, put-downs, and loud, abusive talk.

My immediate goal in counseling was to get her to accept her anger without guilt and thus enable her to deal with it and express it in a more positive and constructive manner, by letting others know when she felt hurt and misunderstood.

However, before the counseling proceeded too far, she went on a thirty day retreat. When she returned, she was the picture of serenity and told me that she no longer needed counseling because her director had taught her to "give it all over to Jesus" and now it was all gone. To myself I said, "Would to God that it were all that easy!"

Her anger, of course, had not been understood and worked through; it had only been suppressed from her consciousness. Beneath the surface it was still very much alive, only now more insidious and more destructive. Later on I counseled some Sisters who worked with Ruth and they found her to be absolutely exasperating. Apparently she was now expressing her anger in a passive-aggressive way. It was all sweetness and light on the surface but in reality she managed to arrange everything to suit her own convenience, no matter how many others were put out and inconvenienced by her actions.

A well-trained spiritual director would have helped her to face her anger and resolve it rather than suppress it. He would have helped her to feel all the pain at the heart of her anger; given her permission to cry, to feel compassion for herself, to forgive herself; and finally, helped her to let go and to make choices for her life with God with a new freedom.

Through the years I have met a number of priests and religious who have testified to their own growth from the psychic pain of shame and guilt to the joy of true self-esteem through the experience of spiritual direction.

4. The Path of Friendship

The final path to a healthy self-esteem is the love experience of a deep friendship, a love relationship with a peer. Few experiences can make me feel more beautiful and secure than the warmth of a dear friend who understands me and cherishes me for myself, just as I am! No matter how badly I may have felt about myself in the past, a genuine love experience can cure my blindness and let me see my beauty and worth. Anyone who has such a friend has the world's best "medicine" for psychic pain.

However, there are two difficulties to be encountered before friendship can be fully efficacious as a path to self-esteem. The first is the enormous difficulty of establishing such an intimate relationship when I have a poor self-concept. The second is the question of sensitive timing.

When I feel very poorly about myself, it is hard for me to believe that someone could love me. "How could this possibly be!" I say to myself. "I have so few talents, so little that's lovable! Once they really get to know me, they are bound to reject me!" This dread is very real! As much as I long for emotional love, it is hard for me even to believe that it is possible for me! So consciously or unconsciously I conclude, "Why risk getting hurt more? Why let myself pretend? It will only hurt worse when they end up rejecting me!"

This fear is so powerful that it seeps through into almost every signal that I send out about myself. My words become self-depreciating. My eye-contact is poor. My mannerisms reflect a person who is withdrawn, uncertain of himself, anxiety-ridden, and all but tongue-tied in social situations. I tend to project my own terrible feelings about myself onto everyone around me, and conclude that this is how they feel about me. I feel that I don't stand a chance! I pull back behind my defenses.

Some years ago, for example, I was counseling Debbie, a Sister in her mid-thirties who hated community gatherings. She felt isolated and alone at them. "Why would anyone care about me?" she would say to herself. "I don't have the kind of personality that attracts others. How could anyone enjoy my company?"

This negative attitude about herself affected her whole manner of dealing with other people. She didn't reach out to the other Sisters, didn't join any group at the large community meetings. She remained isolated and alone, and concluded that no one cared about her. She simply dreaded to go to those meetings.

Then, after five or six months of counseling, when her depression lifted somewhat and she was able to smile and be more affable with the other members of the faculty, one of the Brothers on the faculty began to show her some special attention. He let her know that he enjoyed her and took her out to dinner on several occasions. Fortunately at that stage in her therapy she was able to take the risk that his feelings for her might be real. The relationship grew into a nice friendship with some genuine sharing by both of them.

It was not too long after that that Debbie had to attend a large community meeting. It didn't seem so painful this time. In fact, after it she said to me, "You know, it's really beautiful how warm and friendly our Sisters are. I had such a nice time!" I started to smile. I couldn't resist the temptation to say with tongue-in-cheek: "Debbie, it's remarkable how the whole community has changed during these past few months!" She grinned in recognition. The community hadn't changed of course, but she had! And because she now felt good about herself, she projected these good feelings onto the other Sisters and therefore felt appreciated and admired by them.

The point that is most important here, however, is that the Brother, whose love was a boost to her self-esteem, had been part of the faculty for over two years before he began to notice Debbie's attractiveness. During the time that she felt poorly about herself, she sent out such poor signals, that she apparently was not attractive in his eyes. Nor did she even notice him, not to mention seeing him as a possible friend. It was only when she had enough feeling for herself to take the risk of believing that someone could care for her, it was only then that the friendship process could begin.

Friendship, then, is a high road to self-esteem, but a person often requires some supplementary help in order to walk that road, and he always has to take the risk of getting hurt. The door to my heart through which love can enter and heal me is the same door through which rejection and pain can enter and wound me. If I slam that door closed against possible rejection, I also slam it closed against love and against the exhilarating joys that love can give, including self-esteem.

The second difficulty to be encountered before friendship can heal a wounded self-esteem is the difficulty of achieving a proper sense of timing. When we looked at the basic stages that a person has to go through in order to repair a wounded self-concept, we realized that each stage had to be experienced (not merely recognized and acknowledged) before the person can go on to the next stage. He has to re-experience the painful events which originally distorted his perception before he can really understand those distortions. And he has to forgive those who had hurt him and forgive himself before he can let go of the past and change the false perceptions.

The danger in friendship is that my friend is usually so anxious to help me feel better about myself that he floods me with reassurances and positive affirmation before I am *ready* to receive it and accept it. I appreciate the fact that he means well and I'm grateful for his efforts. But the truth of the matter is that he simply doesn't really understand me. He's reassuring me because he is such a good person but I'm not!

Some years ago, for example, I had skin cancer on my neck. The dermatologist gave me three prescriptions for ointments which had to be applied succesively and only at the proper time. The first one was to kill the old skin and the cancer cells with it. I had to wait for over two weeks until my whole neck was blazing red (the sign that the old skin was dead). Only then could I apply the second salve which encouraged the growth of new skin underneath the old dead skin. And then, finally, a third salve to remove the old dead skin after the new skin was sufficiently developed. The dermatologist stressed that I could abort the whole process if I applied the succeeding salve before the preceding one had accomplished its task. If I had encouraged the growth of the new skin before the old skin was dead, then some of the cancer cells would have remained, and there wouldn't have been a real cure!

The same is true about the process of psychic healing. I must allow each stage of growth sufficient time to accomplish its task before moving on to the next stage. A loving friend can mean well but he can abort the whole healing process by too much affirmation given too soon. As Mary stood by the cross of Jesus and allowed Him to suffer in order to accomplish His life's work, so a true friend allows his beloved to suffer the necessary pains through the stages of growth. It takes a lot of sensitivity and a lot of skill. It takes a lot of love! And most times it is helpful to get the professional advice of a skilled counselor or spiritual director.

Summary

The repairing of a wounded self-esteem is no easy task.
The process is usually long and costly and painful. I first have

to have the dream that self-esteem is a possible goal for those who will struggle to achieve it. And then I must choose the means to gain this new experience of myself and pay the price of going through the process.

The cutting edge by which I replace those warped attitudes about myself is the care and acceptance I receive from a very meaningful person in my present life. Once his or her care gets through to me, I begin to see myself in an entirely new light. I'm good. I'm capable. I have the right to live my own life! The vision is exhilarating!

The difficult part is *letting* the love get through, letting myself believe that someone really cares. Once I open up to love, I automatically open up to the risk of rejection. That is terrifying. It makes me fear that all my old perceptions may be true. I simply have to make myself face this terror and take this risk. The final condition for my new vision is *courage*. Without risk the beautiful healing process cannot proceed, cannot even begin!

What Cardinal Suenens said about the Church of pre-Vatican II applies so aptly here. He was upset that many churchmen *knew* that we needed change desperately, and yet so few had the courage to call for it openly. He summed that situation up in a powerful phrase: "Caution is everywhere. Courage is nowhere! And soon we shall die of prudence!"

Regretfully all too many splendid priests and religious "die" of fear and caution. Their lack of self-esteem robs them of internal freedom. And their fears and timidity hold them back from the relationship and the process that would set them free. If they were to die from a heart attack or cancer, it would be sad. But to "die of prudence" is tragic!

The Fruits of Freedom

However, when I do *dare* to dream the dream and take the risks, the rewards are unbelievably beautiful. I now feel so good about myself that I can easily reach out to others in love. The hesitation and timidity are gone. I project my nice feelings about myself onto you. I'm convinced that you will like me and appreciate my overtures of friendship.

Even signals of possible rejection from you don't threaten me or cause me to retreat. I have such good feelings about myself that I don't make this my problem. I understand that you are fearful. I adjust my degree of self-revelation and closeness to the level where you feel comfortable. I let you know that I don't expect more of you that you feel free to give. I have reverence for your feelings.

I can also let your affirmation and affection touch me and delight me. I can believe that you really see the true me. Thank you very much! I'm so happy that you feel that way! How nice of you to say it!

Comfortable with My Limitations

I'm comfortable with my mistakes and limitations. Of course, I don't know everything! I'm just delighted that I do know an awful lot!

I'm not stupid because I've made some mistakes. I'm human, that's all. I like that! I like the fact that I have a shadow side, that I don't have to be prissy or perfect, or a threat to others.

I gladly give you the "gift" of my mistakes and my needs. I sense that this helps you to be more accepting of your own limitations and needs.

It gives me great joy that I no longer feel the insistent pressure to prove myself. What a relief to know that there is nothing to prove! I'm not on trial. My worth and goodness have already been established. I'm okay!

When you don't seem to appreciate this, I feel badly. I wish you did see me as I really am. But I appreciate the fact that we can see things differently. You have a right to your point of view. I hope someday that you will see me as I see myself. But in the meantime, I don't have to have you like me in order for me to like myself.

I'm comfortable also with my feelings. In fact I'm really pleased that I am a deeply feeling person, not one who is drab and unresponsive. My feelings are like the rainbow. They give beauty and energy to my life.

I'm even proud of those feelings that once made me feel ugly— my anger, my need for your understanding and attention. And because I'm no longer ashamed of them, I can handle them in a healthy way. I tell you that I'm hurt by what you said. Maybe I misunderstood you but this is how I heard it. I don't like being angry at you. I hope we can clear this up. You are no longer threatened by my anger. You are glad also that we can get it out this way.

I'm not afraid to tell you that I need you. I'm not a baby because I feel this way. In fact I feel very happy that I need your attention and care. It proves how much you mean to me. I can tell you that. I can let you know how special you are. I'm free!

An End to Competition

One of my greatest joys is that I no longer feel the insistent burning pressure to compete with you. This is an unbelievable relief. You are not an enemy that I have to conquer in order to feel good about myself. You and I are not in a race. It's not a win-lose situation. We're two separate persons. We're not even on the same track! I can walk and still win, because no one can be me except myself.

The haunting, feverish jealousy is gone! Your victories are *your* victories. They are *not* my defeats! I feel glad for you that you got your doctorate. Congratulations! You must feel so proud. Come on, let's celebrate! This isn't a charade on my part. I really feel good for you. And I feel great about myself that I can enter fully into your joys.

I don't have to have the Bishop notice my work. It's nice if he does. I appreciate it but I don't need his attention to feel good about my work. I already feel good.

I don't need the Provincial to take a special interest in me. I don't have to "dance around" him or her at community meetings. The little boy in me has become a man. The little girl in me has grown up. I'm my own person and happy to be me, whether the Provincial notices me or not.

I no longer feel pushed toward self-punishing ways. If I don't have to get up until ten, I can sleep until ten with perfect peace. I can treat myself to a drink and a nice meal. I can buy myself a new suit before this one becomes threadbare.

When I'm unhappy with my present assignment, I feel free to explore the opportunities for change. Taking the steps to be happy in my work just makes good sense to me. I decide what job would better suit my talents, what training I need for it. I talk to the Provincial. I explain to him the benefits that will come both to the Community and to myself. I set the whole process in motion.

The freedom I feel is absolutely exhilarating. There is no need to pretend that I'm somebody that I'm not; to make believe that I know important people so that I can feel important or to hold onto way-out theories so that I can get attention. I don't need those little games! I don't pretend that I've known something all along when I've just discovered it yesterday. I no longer feel the awful temptation to put you down so that I can feel up. I already feel up. I'm okay!

Compassion for Myself

Perhaps the nicest gift of all is that I can be gentle and compassionate with myself. I no longer have to live up to your expectations in order to keep you from blaming me. If I can do anything to please you, I'm delighted to do so. I reverence you and your dignity. But now I also reverence myself! So, when your expectations are unreasonable, I can gently let you know that. Sorry, I won't be able to pick you up at 2:00 a.m. I'd enjoy being with you, but I'll be dead tired by that time!

If you don't understand this and blame me, I don't buy the guilt. I regret that you don't understand but I have to be true to myself and to my feelings. Far from feeling guilty, I feel great that I'm my own person.

I can also be gentle with myself in my sufferings, even when they are the result of my own faults or my own mistakes. I'm sorry for my faults. But I don't beat myself with a lot of remorse and self-blame. I forgive myself. And I welcome your empathy. I let it touch me and console me.

The Journey's End

All freedom is precious. But this internal freedom—this ability to treasure myself and to be myself without pressure, without fear, without guilt—this is surely the most desirable freedom of all. Once I have experienced its glorious sunshine and wide open spaces, I know with all my heart that the journey and the hardships were all worthwhile! I'm free! I'm free! I want to shout out the good news, as Martin Luther King did, shout for all the world to hear:

FREE AT LAST! FREE AT LAST!
LORD GOD ALMIGHTY, I'M FREE AT LAST!